Sabine Brantl, born in 1969, is a historian and curator at Haus der Kunst in Munich. She freelanced for the Bavarian Television and Jewish Museum Munich and was a research assistant at the Academy of Fine Arts, Munich. On behalf of Haus der Kunst she conceptualised the design of the historical archive in 2004, which she has headed since 2005. Among other things, Sabine Brantl was curator of the exhibition "Histories in Conflict: Haus der Kunst and the Ideological Uses of Art, 1937–1955" (2012) and is responsible for the Archive Gallery, a permanent exhibition room on the history of Haus der Kunst (since 2014).

Sabine Brantl

Haus der Kunst, Munich

A Locality and its History in National Socialism

Published by Haus der Kunst, Munich

Allitera Verlag

Information on the publisher and its programme can be found at:
www.allitera.de

February 2017
Allitera Verlag
A publishing house of Buch&media GmbH, Munich

Translation: Dialogticket, Reinbek b. Hamburg
Cover design using the photograph "Great German Art Exhibition" 1938
Selection of works by Adolf Hitler © Bayerische Staatsbibliothek Munich
Printed in Germany
ISBN 978-3-86906-922-7

Table of Contents

Annex

Foreword

Munich cannot and does not intend to try to escape its historical burden as "Capital of the Movement". The city is aware of this responsibility and faces up to this fact with all its consequences. The central role played by Munich in the birth and rise of National Socialism has long been historical common knowledge. At the turn of the century, anti-Semitic agitation was already present there; this was where the murder of the Jewish Prime Minister, Kurt Eisner, was venerated; where Adolf Hitler celebrated triumphs in gloomy beer cellars and was promoted by sponsors from high society. Munich was the cradle and the control centre of the Nazi Party (NSDAP), was the setting for the failed 9th November 1923 coup and Hitler's trial for high treason that concluded with the most catastrophic error of judgement in German legal history. On 9 November 1938, fifteen years after the march on the Feldherrnhalle, Munich became the starting point for the terror of Kristallnacht, which marked the transition from exclusion, deprivation of rights and persecution, to the planned annihilation of Jews. From the very beginning, this was a place where the evil Nazi spirit was put into practice with the greatest anticipatory fervour. It was in Munich that the first concentration camp was planned and, as early as in March 1933, established at Dachau, in front of the city gates; this was where the Sinti and Roma were systematically registered with murderous intent; this was where the "Brown House" stood and the "Völkischer Beobachter" was published.

At that time, Munich was also made known as the "Capital of German Art". This title was awarded at the ceremony for the laying of the foundation stone for the "Haus der Deutschen Kunst" ("House of German Art") and refers to one of Munich's other features: The city was thus a central location for National Socialist art (re)presentation. This was where racist and nationalist ideals were shown, icons of the "national community" were created, and thus excluding all others who did not – or did not want to – conform to the National Socialists' image of race, self-perception and understanding of art. They were denied the right to exist, first in the realm of "art" and then in reality.

It is all the more important to consciously return this part of history to its authentic location thus giving Haus der Kunst an important place in the topography of the city's remembrance. The efforts on the part of Haus der Kunst to constantly engage in its own past and to use permanent and temporary exhibitions, its website and the present publication, to place this history into a context with the historical and structural inheritance of today's institution, cannot in any way be valued highly enough. This same success is also seen in the other volumes in this series on the University of Music and Performing Arts at Königsplatz (once the "Führer's building" in which the "Munich Agreement" was signed in 1938) and Hildebrandhaus in Bogenhausen (today's "Monacensia"). This makes them an important and necessary component in a cross- city network of remembrance supported by institutions and citizens alike, gradually putting various places and forms of remembrance into an extensive context.

The duty of the city is to encourage and promote such responsible, lively remembrance and educational work, as well as performing this work itself. With the inauguration of the Documentation Centre for the History of National Socialism in 2015 as a place of remembrance and as a central place of historical and political learning on the site of the former "Brown House", we have closed a yawning gap in Munich's landscape of remembrance after many decades. This building, whose existence is not least due to the efforts of committed citizens of our city, makes it unambiguously clear that Munich is facing up to its Nazi past. And this history also specifically includes the so-called honorary title of "Capital of the Movement" and "Capital of German Art".

With this, I wish for this publication a broad readership that engages, in an open and differentiated manner, with those places in our city that bear witness to the regime of terror by the National Socialists and remind us that dealing with the Nazi past remains a perpetual task and moral obligation.

Munich, January 2017

Dieter Reiter
Lord Mayor of Munich, Capital City of Bavaria

Introduction

"Will buildings once misused for ideological or commercial purposes remain tainted for eternity or are buildings stronger than ideologies?" was the question posed by Jacques Herzog and Pierre de Meuron in April 2006 in the context of their exhibition shown at Haus der Kunst. For many years now, contemporary artists and intellectuals have been confronted by the history of the location. Every exhibition of free art is already a comment in itself.
Walls do not bear any guilt but they are places that contain memories and that are permanently linked to specific persons, events and functions.

Haus der Kunst is probably one of the most renowned places for positions in contemporary art. With its programme, this art institution underscores the fact that contemporary art is developing on a complex, global scale and cannot be subject to geographical, conceptual and cultural constraints. At the same time, the building contains reminders of the disastrous combination of art, politics and propaganda in the "Third Reich". Designed in 1933 by Hitler's favourite architect, Paul Ludwig Troost, to present "German" art, "House of German Art" [Haus der Deutschen Kunst] was the first monumental showcase project by the Nazi rulers and a central location for National Socialist propaganda. While the cultural "restoration" of Germany was planned to take place here, artistic freedom and the creative power of the individual ceased to apply. Adolf Hitler inaugurated the building on 18 July 1937 in conjunction with the first "Great German Art Exhibition" [Große Deutsche Kunstausstellung]. In an unprecedented act the very next day, what is known today as classical modernism and its creators were presented in the neighbouring Hofgarten arcades and mocked as "degenerate", sealing their fate for a long time to come. "All of Munich was turned on its head in these days, and not only Munich", wrote John Heartfield from exile in Prague. "The twenty-two stone columns standing in line before the 'Temple of German Art' should have bent over before Hitler's blast of rage and bluster against 'Cultural Bolshevism', against 'artistic infatuation'. He threatened any painters who did not cease 'daring' to paint green skies instead of blue ones, or even blue meadows, that they would be taken to the madhouse or emasculated. The Nazis [...] have castrated the truth, free thought, the development and the lives of many Germans and now the painters and sculptors have been chosen as the next victims."

This is a category of remembrance that must be kept alive. The "Critical Reconstruction" projectlaunched in 2003, which intentionally redirected the questions directed at architecture and legacy, should be seen in this light. When modernism took over the building in the 1950s, it was deemed "de-nazified", internal structural changes were made that were intended to cover up memories of the unpleasant legacy. The red marble cladding of the pillars was whitewashed and the walls and ceilings were installed in the former "Hall of Honour", the centrepiece of the building and the former stage for Hitler's hate-riddled speeches. Since 2003, these subsequent changes are being successively undone in order to uncover the original look.

Making the past visible is one thing, an aggressive engagement with it is another. When the "Utopia Station" group project was installed in Munich Station in autumn 2004, an invisible pack of German shepherd dogs barked at visitors from a noise installation by Christian Boltanski, right at the entrance to the building. A banner by the American painter Leon Golub flew from one of the flag poles in front of the building where the swastika flag was raised for the first time in 1937. Utopia, the concept of the best of all possible worlds, had deconstructed the National Socialists' trimmed, inhuman world view with its own weapons and unhinged it.

But discussion should not be limited to the authentic location. While the building is mentioned in most publications on National Socialist architecture, art and cultural policy, there were until now no monographs that dealt in-depth with the history of the origins, significance and impact of the former "House of German Art". The present publication is intended to close this gap and at the same time encourage an ongoing engagement with the controversial issue – currently still being discussed – of how to deal with art and architecture in the "Third Reich". For this book, it was possible to access documents that until 2004 were stored forgotten in a room in the cellar of the building – today's Historical Archive of Haus der Kunst; documents show, among other things, how Haus der Kunst was organised at the time of the "Great German Art Exhibitions" and what decisive role Hitler played in these propaganda shows. The book centres on the building's

Nazi past although the history of the building's predecessor, the Glass Palace which burnt down in 1931, as well as the decades and cultural reactions post 1945 are also discussed. This seems to be the correct focus, as well as with regard to the 70th anniversary in July 2007 which was the occasion for the first edition of this publication. In order to be able to determine one's own position, the starting point must be known and history must be subjected to critical scrutiny.

My heartfelt thanks goes out to the Culture Department of Munich, Capital City of the State of Bavaria, which provided financial support for the project and Chris Dercon who was director of Haus der Kunst from 2003 to 2011. Furthermore, I would like to express my thanks to all the staff of the archives and libraries who facilitated this work with their professional assistance. Most of all, I would like to thank Dr Ralf Peters of the Central Institute for Art History, Bernhard Grau of the Archives of the Bavarian State, Munich and Elisabeth Angermair, Anton Löffelmeier and Angela Stilwell of the Munich City Archive. For providing me with important leads, organisational assistance and constructive criticism, I express my gratitude to Klaus Bäumler, Anthea Niklaus, Dr León Krempel and Swantje Grundler, as well as Marco Graf von Matuschka, Anton Köttl and Iris Ludwig at Haus der Kunst. I would like to thank the Künstlerverbund im Haus der Kunst (formerly Ausstellungsleitung) e. V. and Helmut Kästl of Münchner Secession for generously giving permission to use some of their photographs.

Munich, January 2017 *Sabine Brantl*

1 A new Glass Palace

1.1 The Glass Palace fire

On the night of 5–6 June 1931, Munich's Glass Palace at the Old Botanical Garden was completely destroyed by fire. The fire alarm at the corner of Karlsstrasse/Arcisstrasse was set off at 3.26 a.m. By the time the first fire engine arrived at the scene, the central section and the right wing of the exhibition hall were already in flames.[1] Five minutes later further fire engines were requested. Despite the massive use of fire-fighting equipment, the teams of fire fighters only succeeded in bringing the fire under control after eight and a half hours. All that remained was a field of smoking ruins, uncountable numbers of shards of shattered and molten glass and the bare skeleton of iron columns and beams. Apart from an insignificant fraction of paintings and sculptures, some 3000 works of art had been destroyed including most of the lifetime achievements of the Swiss painter Cuno Amiet, a member of "Die Brücke" and all 110 paintings of a special exhibition of German romantic artists from Caspar David Friedrich to Moritz von Schwind.

The Munich art exhibition had been opened only four days previously, on 1 June 1931 in the presence of the Bavarian Minister of Education and the Arts, Dr Franz Goldenberger, and many prominent politicians, businessmen and artists. As with every year, the collective show by the artists' associations formed the start of Munich's summer of art.[2] The exhibition displayed works by members of the traditional "Münchener Künstler-Genossenschaft" [Munich art cooperative] and the "Secession", which represented moderate modernism and in this year welcomed French and Italian artists such as Giorgio de Chirico, Raoul Dufy and Maurice Utrillo as guests. Smaller groupings such as Luitpoldgruppe, the Bavarian Arts and Crafts Association and the "Juryfreie", in which the avant-garde gathered from the beginning of the 1930s onwards, were also represented.[3] Walter Zimmermann, the general director of the art exhibitions in the Glass Palace, and art critic Georg Jakob Wolf had additionally brought together a top-class show of romantic artists from German museums and private holdings that was housed in three rooms in the southern section of the central building and was intended to be the main attraction of the Glass Palace exhibition of 1931. The exhibition got off to a very promising start, there were unusually high numbers of visitors even in the first few days. In addition, the spring show by the "Münchener Neue Secession e. V." was coming to an end, an association formed in 1913 that had held exhibitions on their own initiative since 1920 in the separate west wing of the Glass Palace which had its own entrance. Their exhibits were almost completely destroyed by fire.

The Glass Palace fire did not deeply shock just a few people. The "Flames of the Munich Glass Palace" were described by Eugen Roth, who had been an eye-witness of the night of the fire, writing from the perspective of 1971, as "a beacon marking disasters to come" and as "one of the first burnt marks on the face of our city".[4] The press spoke of a "national catastrophe", an irreplaceable loss "suffered by Bavaria and the entire world of culture [...]".[5] Only a few hours after the fire, blocks of molten structural glass and the remains of a ceramic bowl from the handicraft section of the Glass Palace display in the museum of city history at St. Jakobsplatz that had become interfused with drops of glass and ash.[6] Expressions of sympathy came from other European countries and the United States. In Munich itself, relief efforts set in and spontaneously organised benefit events were held to assist the artists who had suffered losses. Celebrities from cultural and intellectual life also put themselves at the service of "support for Glass Palace artists". Thomas Mann, for example, held a public reading on 5th July 1931 from his novel "Joseph and his Brothers" at Munich University's main lecture theatre.[7]

The cause of the catastrophic fire was never firmly established. Munich city council also had to deal with this question. In an emergency motion, the NSDAP grouping within the city council demanded an in-depth inquiry into the circumstances of the fire alarm. SS men claimed to have seen "a small strip of fire in the Glass Palace" at around three in the morning while they were on patrol at the corner of Brienner Strasse and Arcisstrasse. They claimed that the fire alarm was not working making it impossible to raise the alarm. They then notified staff at the main fire station both by telephone and a runner from the Brown House but they did not believe the messages. During the city council meeting on 9 June 1931, Hermann Esser, one of the NSDAP's most aggressive demagogues and editor of the "Illustrierter

Munich's Glass Palace the day after the catastrophic fire

Beobachter" since 1926, accused the police that "although they otherwise took every available opportunity, ganged up in groups of ten or more, to strip a National Socialist of his brown shirt if he dared to go for a walk dressed in it, they do not have any resources to keep Munich's Glass Palace permanently under observation". In his closing remarks that were saturated with fierce outbursts against the "shambles" in Munich, he placed the blame for the fire on the government and demanded the resignation of those responsible. The motion was rejected by the majority.[8] According to police investigations, the night watchmen Schellerer and Bäuml as well as the private fireman Reiter were in the building at the time the fire broke out. "The night watchman Schellerer was doing his rounds [...] at 3.20 a.m. he punched the fourth check in Room 28 on the watchman's clock he carried with him. On his way to Room 32 from there Schellerer heard a noise on the walkways above him that he initially did not pay any attention to. Apparently he was of the opinion that martens were running around upstairs, which had often been the case in the past. But the next instant, however, he saw a bright light from his position in Hall 33 in the direction of Room 44. He ran through Room 44 and from there to Room 62. He got as far as the entrance to that Hall where he saw burning parts of the muslin coverings and pieces of burning wood falling down. Schellerer had the impression that a fire must have broken out above Room 62. He ran back through Room 44 to Room 1 and the forecourt. Here he saw that the stairway leading up from the forecourt to the copying room was in flames. However, the flames had mostly caught hold of the two chambers adjacent to the stairs; from here the flames spread upwards. The two chambers were used by master painter Beyhl to store materials. Schellerer ran to the guardroom to wake Bäuml and Reiter. The private fireman Reiter then immediately pulled the fire alarm in the forecourt next to the main entrance. During his interrogation, Reiter stated that he had the impression when coming out of the guardroom that the fire must have started at the chambers next to the stairway as the fire had burnt its way up the wooden walls and had also taken hold of the staircases. While Bäuml and Reiter were still able to escape from the building through the main entrance, Schellerer had to use the emergency exit in the east wing due to the explosive spreading of the fire. The firm alarm from the outside came virtually at the same time as the alarm by the private fireman Reiter".[9] The police authorities stated the cause of the fire to be self-ignition of rolls of muslin soaked in varnish, turpentine and oil paint that were stored in one of two closets to the west of the main entrance. The evening before the fire, employees of master painter Beyhl had adjusted the colour of the wall paint. As the Glass Palace did not have electric lighting, such work could only be carried out between the close of the exhibition and nightfall. In the third room of the exhibition of romantic artists located in the central hall, wood panelling was painted over with grey oil paint that was wiped off again as the shade did not meet the expectations of the exhibition organisers. For this purpose, cloths made of muslin steeped in turpentine were used, that were subsequently stored in a chamber next to the main entrance. "The high temperature prevailing in the Glass Palace after the warm days", the police report continues, "presumably supported the process of self-ignition [...] The catastrophic extent and the destruction of the entire building complex was extraordinarily favoured by dividing up and separating off the individual rooms with wooden walls. The greatest danger, however, came from the textile coverings on the walls and ceilings to soften the light or allow it to shine in the right way. When the initial fire broke a few panes of glass the draught was free to circulate which led to the fire spreading out in a flash. Intentional arson was ruled out: "When investigating the cause of the fire there was no lack of communications and suspicions that pointed to intentional arson. Even the organisers of the exhibition reckoned with the possibility that the known disagreements within the art community, the rejection of some artists, the radical opinions of some of those rejected, etc., could have been the incitement for laying the fire intentionally. The police's call in the press for information from the general public led to individuals being suspected. None of the investigations in this direction gave rise to any facts or indications of intentional arson."[10] An assessment carried out by the forensic chemistry investigation unit of the medical committee of Munich University also came to this conclusion.[11] This was contradicted in August 1931 by the assessment carried out by Munich's building authority, according to which the Glass Palace was destroyed by arson. In his extensive dossier, senior councillor Neithard pointed out the significant difference between "oily cotton waste or oily cleaning rags used in industrial machinery and rags dirtied with oil paint that probably come into existence from time to time in the course of any painter-decorator's business when he has to wipe freshly applied oil paint off again. It is probably attributable to this difference that self-ignition of rags besmirched with oil paint is just about unknown among artistic painters and painter-decorators while the ignition of cotton waste soaked in oil is not an uncommon experience at all." Self-ignition was improbable in this case if only because the muslin rolls were so thoroughly clogged up with oil paint that the paint was more likely to have an "inhibiting effect [...] on heating and ignition". After reviewing the available witnesses' statements, there was no doubt in Neithard's mind that it was "intentional arson" that started "from the quite hidden iron emergency staircase that could be reached from the street" on the west side of the entrance – the place where the fire was first discovered by night watchman Schellerer.[12] The government of Upper Bavaria followed the line of argument of the building authority.[13] A perpetrator was never identified.

An era in Munich's exhibition history came to an end along with the Glass Palace. A series of significant exhibitions held since the 1860s had developed the building into a cultural centre and a decisive factor in Munich's reputation as a city of art. The Glass Palace was originally purpose-built in 1853/54 for the "General Exhibition of German

Industrial and Trade Products". On 2 August 1853, King Maximilian II had given orders for the staging of "a Customs Union industrial exhibition" the following year. Bavaria had been a member of the German Customs Union since 1833 which held a loose sequence of public exhibitions. This exhibition of achievements, designed based on the model of the first World Exhibition of 1851 and offering a great variety of products ranging from steam engines to utensils of all kinds, was intended to act as an important stimulus for the still nascent Bavarian industry. As no suitable building was available in Munich, a new construction was planned. The Dultplatz in Maximiliansplatz, Maximilianstrasse and the Royal Botanical Gardens between Sophienstrasse and Elisenstrasse were discussed among others as various potential locations. Due to its favourable position in close vicinity to the main station and the city centre, the Botanical Gardens were chosen. This was by all means a controversial choice which led the director of the Botanical Gardens, Karl Friedrich von Martius, to resign. The short planning period from August 1853 to its inauguration in July 1854 was decisive for the design and construction of the new exhibition hall. And so King Maximilian II commissioned August von Voit, who had already proven his abilities as an architect of the Neue Pinakothek (which was destroyed in the Second World War) by constructing a glass exhibition hall modelled after London's Crystal Palace of 1851. Only with the innovative solution of a glass-iron construction made using prefabricated parts, was it possible to start building in more than one place at once and to be finished within nine months. Finished components made of cast iron and glass were manufactured by the Cramer-Klett factory in Nuremberg and delivered by train. In order to facilitate the transportation of the solid iron parts, railway track was laid from Munich main station to the building site at Sophienstrasse/Elisenstrasse. In comparison to London's Crystal Palace, August von Voit's plans seem more minimalistic and more progressive in its concept; he raised the design to an "aesthetic category" thus making it an outstanding example of modern architectural engineering extending far beyond the 1850s.[14] It was not until half a century later that this route was consistently pursued by architects such as Walter Gropius and Ludwig Mies van der Rohe. For the interior, August von Voit designed three fountains to take the humidity out of the air and placed corresponding installations in the garden. The richly decorated main fountain in the central nave was removed in 1897 at the application of the central committee of the VII International Art Exhibition to make space for a temple to be built. The dismantled fountain was stored for decades on the grounds of the Old Botanical Gardens and survived the fire of 1931. Since 1974 it has been located at Weißenburger square in Munich's Haidhausen district. It is the only work by August von Voit which has survived in Munich.[15]

Industry and Trade Exhibition, 1854

Although the Glass Palace was planned to be a temporary building, a decision was made after the end of the industrial exhibition to leave the building standing for the time being. The original idea of converting parts of the architecture – 234 metres in length and 67 metres in width – into a greenhouse were discarded as being too expensive. Following plans aired from time to time to use the building as a department store, a covered market or swimming pool, the Glass Palace was put under the administration of the government of Upper Bavaria as a state building in 1855. It was not until autumn 1856 when an offer came in from the Belgian consul "to purchase the industrial exhibition building for demolition", Maximilian II finally spoke out in favour of retaining the Glass Palace.[16] And so the Glass Palace became a general centre for exhibitions and other events that had great power to attract visitors even from beyond the borders of Bavaria. It was home to exhibitions of pedigree dogs and agricultural equipment, flower shows, festive banquets, military exercises and much more. One sensation was the "International Electricity Exhibition" of 1882 organised by Oskar von Miller, where one of the attractions was the transmission of electricity from a power station in Miesbach to Munich, a distance of more than 57 kilometres. It was in 1858 that the Glass Palace opened its doors to art for the first time. The "German General and Historical Art Exhibition" on the occasion of the 50th anniversary of the Academy of Fine Arts was so successful

Munich's Glass Palace, around 1890

that it was followed up by further events. "The First International Art Exhibition" of 1869 entered art history as an event at which Gustav Courbet and young Leibl caused a sensation and that made Munich a centre of modernism.[17] From 1889 onwards, the Glass Palace was then used almost exclusively for art exhibitions; the building became the most important and the biggest forum for exhibitions in Munich. This was where, among others, the annual exhibitions by Munich's artists' associations and, as of 1879, the International Art Exhibitions, held every four years, took place. The glass-iron architecture provided sufficient space of more than 12,000 square metres and an easily reachable location at the heart of the city for these sales events with up to 3000 paintings, sculptures and craftwork products. This enormous variety did, however, lead to considerable fluctuations in quality and times when the building was empty. The emphasis was increasingly placed on "official" art, characterised by traditionalism. It was not without a little irony that Julius Wolfgang Schuelein, born in Munich in 1881 and who participated in the Glass Palace exhibitions himself, decades later recalled these large-scale events in which conservatives set the tone: "There were huge pictures such as the Battle at Gravelotte or, representing French art, a Rochegrosse with hundreds of life-size nude women, a picture that was presumably called the Fall of Babylon. Or you saw monks enjoying the delights of alcohol or red and violet ecclesiastics, playing chess or charming peasant girls with sentimental but robust peasant lads. Or sadistically exciting things like some tsarina or other having naked women freeze to death in the snow, or beautiful red-headed witches being inspected for witch marks. Alongside these, some Bavarian or Italian landscapes, always the same ones, time after time, by the same painter. And a room with Böcklin pictures and rooms in semi-darkness with old chests and velvet decorations in which the painter-prince Lenbach presented his most recent portraits of famous or rich people or envied female beauties. The first upheaval in Munich came with the formation of the Secession that threw historical and genre painting overboard and mainly cultivated an insipid naturalism [...] It was in the Secession that I first had the childish pleasure of exhibiting. And I was then part of the show when the "New Secession" was formed in 1913 ... Once when the New Secession [...] was exhibiting, the pictures, that almost everyone today would consider to be very conservative [...] unleashed a storm of indignation and it was written that the painters should have hung themselves up instead of their pictures."[18]

At the beginning of the 20th century, the Glass Palace, as an exhibition hall, was far from uncontroversial. Although extensive repair work had been carried out in 1913, there were increasingly frequent calls to replace the building with a new one. "What should happen to it?", Wilhelm von Hausenstein asked in the "Münchner Neueste Nachrichten" in 1918. "The interior of the glass-iron building is, without doubt, relatively functional and pleasant. The exterior is, however, no architectural ornament [...] For years now, there have been justified discussions on whether to demolish the Glass Palace, also from the perspective of the layout of the park. It would not be a disaster if a symbol of an era drawing to a close were to be replaced by a symbol of creativity that is yet to come."[19] A modern conversion of the ageing hall was also debated. The result of a competition organised in 1922 for the architectural restructuring of the Old Botanical Gardens that was to include the Glass Palace was only one of several projects that failed to be implemented on account of the tense financial situation.[20] But there was no end to the discussions about whether to retain or demolish the Glass Palace. The catastrophic fire in the night of 5–6 June 1931 brought this dispute to a sudden end.

Annual Munich Exhibition, 1890

1.2 Adolf Abel's preliminary project

After the Glass Palace fire, the Munich Artists' Cooperative, the Secession and the New Secession formed the "Ausstellungsleitung e. V." (Exhibition Administration) in order to organise an exhibition to replace the destroyed "Great Munich Art Exhibition". The rooms required were provided by Oskar von Miller in the recently completed library building of the Deutsches Museum. The exhibition was opened on 15 July 1931 and there were plans for the Deutsches Museum to house it once again the following year. People were probably aware that this was only a provisional solution and a new replacement building for the Glass Palace was inevitable – despite the precarious budgetary situation. For the time being, the commitment of the Ministry of Education and the Arts was revealed in a five-page circular sent out in mid-July to Munich's artistic groups, the Academy of Fine Arts and other opinion leaders in the fields of fine arts, architecture and the world of museums. The recipients were asked to put forward "which functions the new building should perform, how much space is needed and what form – closed in area or pavilions – is desired". Furthermore, the question was raised as to whether "in the more distant future, there will even still be a regular need for large, representative exhibitions in the sense and scope of the previous Glass Palace exhibitions." Only when the results of this survey were available would it be possible to examine "whether these requirements, taking into account aspects of urban development and traffic needs, could be met at the present location or, something that can hardly be presumed, whether if necessary, another, better solution would have to be found."[21] The question remained unanswered as to "whether, when and how" it would be possible to make the necessary funds available for the new building. It was the same situation with the possibility of holding a contest for ideas for which the ministry had still not given a statement. Those surveyed generally agreed that the previous location in the Old Botanical Gardens should be retained. The new exhibition building should also be usable all year round thanks to a new heating system and the installation of electrical light. The concept of a public café-restaurant with a share of the garden was also welcomed. Likewise, sufficient parking space for visitors from outside the city was another request.[22] The artist groups emphatically demanded a public competition that, in their opinion, constituted the only and sole guarantee of a satisfactory solution with regard to the design. As financing had not been secured up to that point, the Ministry of Education and the Arts decided to first have a preliminary design for a new building drafted that could be used both as an exhibition building and as a concert hall. This was hoped to bring in a larger subsidy from the city especially as Munich urgently needed a music hall. In November 1931, the Bavarian Ministry of Education and the Arts commissioned the architect Adolf Abel with preparing the preliminary design.[23] This was a formally consistent decision as the architect had been promised the next major state building in 1930 when he was appointed the successor to Theodor Fischer's professorship. According to the characterisation by the architectural historian Winfried Nerdinger, Adolf Abel, born in Paris in 1882 was "indeed controversial, but one of the most interesting architectural personalities seen in Germany in the first half of the century."[24] Prior to his appointment at Munich Technical University, Adolf Abel worked as director of urban development in Cologne and left a decisive mark on the face of the "New Cologne" with his buildings in the Konrad Adenauer era. His main works include the new university buildings' complex, a functionally unpretentious building that consciously dispensed with elaborate decoration, as well as the trade fair area in Cologne-Deutz completed in 1928 for the occasion of the International Press Exhibition, "a characteristic mixture of motives from the New Objectivity movement with traditional down-to-earth forms" for Adolf Abel.[25] The decision by the Ministry of Education and the Arts to assign the preliminary design of an exhibition building to Adolf Abel set off a wave of protests and verbal aggression that would have been difficult to surpass in terms of virulence and personal insult. The attack against the plans by the Ministry of Education and the Arts was led primarily by the artists' associations and, in particular, the community of architects with the support of the local press. The Federal Association of Bavarian Architects announced "actions of strongest protest" if the Ministry of Education and the Arts did not reconsider its decision not to hold a public competition. "The thought that this task would, like so many others in this time of adversity, should fall into the hands of an official with a fixed salary is downright incomprehensible in light of the appalling plight of the liberal professions" claimed the 30 November 1931 issue of "Münchner Neueste Nachrichten".[26] The "Völkischer Beobachter" took on a much fiercer tone and did not shy from attacking Adolf Abel as a person: "They all act as if they were oh so Bavarian but when they have to put their empty words into practice they regularly come up with a loser. It's all a façade. A façade."[27] In particular, Eugen Hönig, First President of the Munich Artists Cooperative and Chair of the Federation of German Architects made himself Abel's personal opponent. The irreconcilable position of this member of the National Socialist party and later president of the Reich Chamber of Fine Arts led to the right-wing parties represented in the state parliament taking an interest in the matter and feeling called to become advocates of Munich's artists' associations. The persistent protests ultimately achieved their goal. By resolution of the state parliament of 10 March 1932, the official announcement was published on 31 July 1932 on the "holding of a contest for ideas for an art exhibition building in Munich." Admission extended to all "German-speaking architects born or resident in Bavaria". The deadline for submission ended on 15 November 1932.[28]

In the meantime, Adolf Abel's preliminary draft had been completed and presented to the general public in the exhibition pavilion on Elisenstrasse. The model and plans showed a solution compromising between a large hall and division into pavilions that was, as the architect put it in his explanatory report, a "supplement to the existing urban development" located in the south-western part of the Old Botanical Gardens.[29] The centre of the floor plan was taken up by what was to be known as the "Hall of Honour" – it was from this "key room" that you walked to the side wings and to the directly connected main hall, that could be converted into a concert hall for 2000 people thanks to the incorporation of a moving stage. The interior rooms were developed in such a way that the old Glass Palace returned in the form of a rectangular glass body. This glass body surrounded by an outer frame and starting at a higher level than the picture walls guaranteed favourable light at every time of the day all year round. An electrical lighting system additionally made it possible to regulate the brightness separately in each individual room. A network of "sockets" set in the floor at regular intervals facilitated the placing of partition walls at will, thus permitting the best possible configuration of the rooms. The functional design of the new building would permit the predominant use of reinforced concrete. The idea was to use a "nobler material" for the main entrance, the side entrances and the spacious exhibition courtyard with the café-restaurant. As expected, Munich's artists' associations reacted sceptically to the presented draft; they did, however, generally refrain from polemically worded statements in view of the imminent competition. There was mainly a positive response from the professional journals. Werner Hegemann, co-editor of the monthly architecture journal "Monatshefte für Baukunst und Städtebau" even congratulated the City of Munich "that it had known how to appoint the right man to the right

Adolf Abel, preliminary design for the new art exhibition building at the Old Botanical Garden, 1932

position untroubled by parochial prejudices".[30] Surprisingly, Munich's local press mostly turned out to be supportive. Alexander Heilmeyer, editor of "Münchner Neueste Nachrichten" and, as of 1937 editor of the Nazi magazine "Die Kunst im Dritten Reich", should be mentioned as representative. One of the things he appreciated most about the project was "that it is modest in its dimensions and, instead of a brash monumentality, aimed at a cultivated intimacy that corresponded to the cosy, open, southern German urban setting"[31] This meant that, in his opinion, the preliminary project by Adolf Abel offered "an excellent basis for everything else" (which was a reference to the competition that had long been imposed).

Even though such high-calibre personalities as Richard Riemerschmid, Hans Döllgast and Karl Hocheder participated, the competition did not bring forward any result that was worth implementing. More than just a few of the 499 submissions in total were merely variations on the draft prepared by Adolf Abel or presented museum architecture, taking themes from historicism. First prize was awarded to the Augsburg architects Clemens Böhm and Eduard Feldpausch for a draft that the jury judged to be "very balanced, attractive and functional in its overall arrangement".[32] The government building officers Karl Hocheder and Karl Badberger received second prize, with their proposed project revealing a conspicuous affinity to Adolf Abel's project.[33] In mid-December, the Ministry of Education and the Arts in turn commissioned Adolf Abel to produce a second, modified preliminary design.[34] The concept of also being able to use the building as a concert hall was finally shelved. Moreover, an exhibition area totalling 8000 square metres was now deemed sufficient – which was nevertheless a third smaller than the old Glass Palace. The structural work was scheduled to begin in late summer 1933. Progress was also being made with regard to financing, even if it had not quite been finalised. The Bavarian State and the Reich Ministry of the Interior had undertaken to provide funds. In addition, Dr. Franz Koempel and his wife Bertha, New York residents and the owners of today's "Waldberta" scholarship villa at Lake Starnberg, donated a total of over 1,000,000 dollars for the promotion of the annual art events in the new exhibition building.[35] The so-called "seizure of power" by the National Socialists brought this project to a stop. While construction work was just about to start in spring 1933, there were, however, "really monumental plans" under discussion at this point that Hitler was entertaining with regard to the new building.[36] Eugen Hönig now started calculating his chances again. His statement against Abel's draft, which he had not seen himself, is really a rhetorical example of what form any argument against unwelcome competition would take in coming years, particularly with regards to the party and state: "I hope and expect", he informed the new Nazi Minister of Education and the Arts, Hans Schemm, on 18th March 1933 "that, under the new regime of concentrating national forces in an art exhibition building in Munich, an externally visible symbol of really national artistic intent will be created and nothing foreign and alien to the city, as Professor Abel would presumably build considering his all-too-familiar activities in Cologne. I believe that there is all the more reason, as surely the Reich Chancellor surely has an interest of his own, that the art exhibition building of the greatest German art metropolis should become a hallmark of a particularly impressive symbol of German civilising intent, mindful of the fact that it was from this place that the national uprising had its origins. [...] In support of my statement, I would like to not leave it unmentioned that I am a party member and, consequently, I thoroughly also share the cultural perspective of the concept of art as propagated by the "Völkischer Beobachter". I would be pleased to be consulted in an advisory capacity in all issues relating to my profession in the narrower sense or of an artistic nature, as my opposition over many years to the ruling powers is adequate legitimation alone for what I aim and have always aimed to achieve."[37]

The courageous attempt on the part of Richard Hendschel, an art expert in the Ministry of Education and the Arts, to win over Hitler personally for Abel's project should be mentioned in this context. To this end, he had the model of the exhibition building taken to the villa of the publisher Hugo Bruckmann, one of the most influential patrons of Adolf Hitler. "But", Richard Hendschel wrote in his memoirs, "it wasn't even possible to persuade Hitler to even have a quick look at the model. At that point I was still not aware that Hitler was already determined to transfer responsibility for construction to Professor Troost and that the space had already been designated to it. Abel's model was not returned to the artist and has disappeared somewhere. And so this was how the monumental building "The House of German Art" now came into being at Prinzregentenstrasse, erected on very difficult ground and at tremendous cost."[38]

2 The “Führer’s First Builder”

2.1 Paul Ludwig Troost

“Troost had not participated in the tendered competition for a new building. His style was not very well received at that time [...] Only the Führer was familiar with these sheets of paper in which the pencil of the architect of German art had drafted a building: modest, clear, exuding great dignity and strict transcendence free of pathos, as appropriate to the German character”.[39] Even long after the “House of German Art” had been completed, the press (which had already been brought in line with official policy) recalled at regular intervals the origins of the buildings, as the “Neue Münchener Tageblatt” did in 1938. Special importance was given to Paul Ludwig Troost and his close relationship with Hitler. Emulating the omnipresent National Socialist propaganda, the image of an architect was conjured up who, even in the so-called “time of decay” of the Weimar Republic, consistently and irrespective of any appreciation received, held on tightly to a style of architecture that “never lost touch with national soil” and only through recognition by Adolf Hitler was to become the guiding figure for a whole generation of artists. Who was this architect who entered the cultural history of National Socialism as the “Führer’s First Builder”? What course had his professional career taken before he attracted Hitler’s attention and ultimately commissioned him with the first representative building of the “Third Reich”?

Born in Elberfeld in 1878, Paul Ludwig Troost had been a resident in Munich since 1900. After his studies of architecture at Darmstadt Technical University, Troost took on the running of the planning office of Martin Dülfer, the most important Art Nouveau architect in Munich, before becoming self-employed as a freelance architect.[40] Together with Dülfer, Heinrich Vogeler und Rudolf Alexander Schröder, this young architect worked on the design of the famous residence of the publisher Alfred Walter Heymel in Leopoldstrasse which also housed the editorial rooms of “Die Insel’s” monthly journal of aesthetic and literary matters.

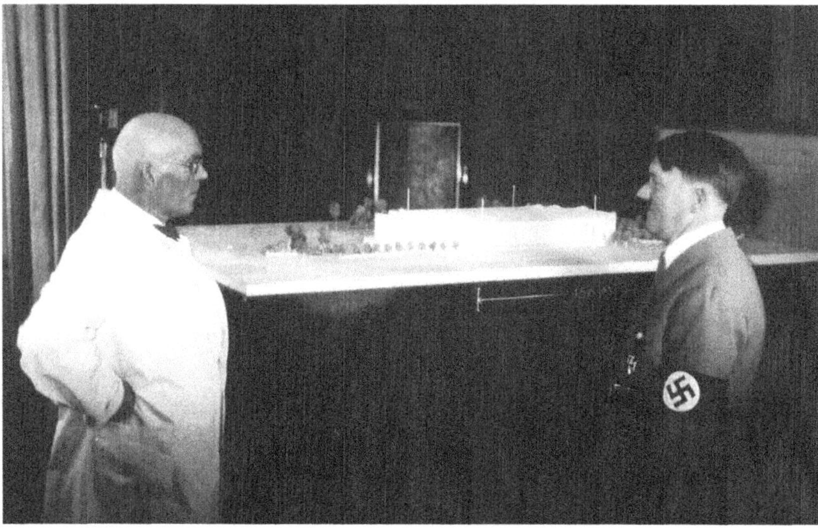

In front of the model of the "House of German Art": Paul Ludwig Troost and Adolf Hitler at the Troost Atelier, Theresienstrasse 148, in 1933

The interior completed according to drafts by Rudolf Alexander Schröder caused a sensation with its novel, emphatically plain design and was discussed far and wide. "It is a flat, dozens of them have been described in these pages over the years; the generic term just won't fit this one," wrote the famous art critic Julius Meier-Graefe in the magazine "Dekorative Kunst" in 1901. "The strange thing about the flat is the lack of amateurism. Specifically the one thing that impresses amateurs most about modernism, the new ornamentism, is disregarded here in favour of a cool certainty, hardly any artist can bring himself to apply."[41] Without doubt, the plain classicising style of the "Insel" flat and the concept emerging at the turn of the century of a building as "a complete work of art", in which every detail should express the distinctive style of its inhabitants (one could think of the Villa Stuck built in 1897/98) paved the way for Paul Ludwig Troost's further work. This was clearly seen in his first independent project, the villa of the landscape painter Benno Becker in Munich-Bogenhausen, the entire interior of which was designed by Troost himself.[42] The palazzo-style building, the construction of which was completed in late summer 1904 shows design features that already give an impression of Troost's late work in the 1930s. The function of classical building elements limited to decoration such as stone columns and plinths, their reduced antique styling and the motive of the central hall with panelled ceiling inside are also found in the "House of German Art".

Paul Ludwig Troost had established himself as a sought-after architect already in the early years of his professional work, drawing the attention of Munich's high society primarily through his elegant spatial creations. His clients included, among others, the composer Felix von Rath, the private lecturer Hans Kupelwieser and the publishers Elsa and Hugo Bruckmann, in whose salon Paul Ludwig Trosst was a frequent guest.[43] Troost also participated in exhibitions on many an occasion to present his furnishings to a wider public. For example, his work was represented at the World Exhibitions in Brussels and Gent in 1910 and 1913. But it was his cooperation with Norddeutscher Lloyd, which did not begin until 1912, that gained him international fame. As artistic director and successor of Bruno Paul, he furnished virtually all the huge ocean liners of this Bremen-based shipping company until 1930.[44] He designed representative interiors for hundreds of rooms – from the pattern of carpets to table silver, from the staircase banister to the most diverse light fittings. The generously dimensioned arrangements of rooms, mostly merging into each other over several storeys, form atmospheric ensembles of furniture, colour and décor that in their luxurious solidity and in a mixture of conservative and modernistic elements had to "represent German culture in the world in the most dignified way possible," was the way in which art historian Franz Arens characterised this "steamer style" which linked modern technology with the demands of representation and self-portrayal.[45] With this, Troost moved on to become the leading ship interior designer of the 1920s. The social and political upheavals following the First World War, however, did not have any impact on his work. Between 1914 and 1918, Toost, who had been exempted from military service on account of a heart condition, dedicated himself to expanding war ships. In 1917, he was appointed professor by King Ludwig III of Bavaria. He continued to see one of his main tasks as "awakening the artistic interest of the well-off public".[46] "You are well aware that my main aim is to produce good art and to provide clients with tasteful and sound work and it has always been my experience that you ultimately end up using the finest materials in this respect because the finished work is then the best advertisement," he wrote in a letter to Hans Barth in 1926.[47] In order to live up to this claim, it was necessary to have – alongside the required large amount of funds – a well-functioning staff of employees and qualified workshops.

Paul Ludwig Troost usually entrusted implementation of artistic room decoration to Munich-based colleagues such as Josef Wackerle, Alfred Hagel, Angelo Jank, Eduard Thöny or Hans Gött, who were from the circle of the traditionalist "Secession" and whom he treated as friends.[48] Even the companies that Troost commissioned for his immense creative activities were mainly located in Munich. For Nymphenburger Porzellanmanufaktur he designed tableware and porcelain sculptures starting sometime before 1904,[49] he had already been closely associated with Vereinigte Werkstätten since his time with Martin Dülfer.[50]

A "diplomat's desk" on display at the premises of Vereinigte Werkstätten was also said to have been the one Adolf Hitler absolutely wanted to acquire in 1926 and that drew his persistent interest to his later showcase architect.[51] The first personal encounter between Hitler and Troost took place four years later at Hugo Bruckmann's house. Hitler had asked the publisher to arrange this meeting. Bruckmann's villa at Karolinenplatz had developed into the focal point for Munich's reactionary circles from the 1920s onwards. Later, party bigwigs like Rudolf Hess, Baldur von Schirach and Alfred Rosenberg were received here. Hugo and Elsa Bruckmann, themselves "old party members", promoted and supported Hitler financially and introduced him to important contacts in society. Hitler approached Paul Ludwig Troost with a very specific request. In July 1930, the NSDAP had purchased the classicistic "Palais Barlow" from Elise Barlow, a widow of independent means, for a price of 805,864 gold marks.[52] The building that stood between Königsplatz and Karolinenplatz in Brienner Strasse was now to be redesigned as a representative administrative building. The party headquarters, up to that time located in a back building of Schellingstrasse, had become too small

Becker Villa, around 1904/05

due to the growing numbers of members. In addition, the new location in one of the most elegant residential areas of Munich was to make the party "respectable" and attractive for voters from more affluent classes. The close vicinity to Königsplatz, a square that the National Socialists occupied as a party forum in 1933 almost certainly also played a role in the choice of building. When redesigning the "Brown House" (as the building was called from now on with reference to the colour of the party uniforms), Paul Ludwig Troost fully implemented Hitler's ideas. Pathetic monumentality and a solemn-chilly atmosphere of the rooms was characteristic of the style used in the interior. A special emphasis was placed on the foyer (guarded day and night by SS men), for which the architect produced detailed drafts for the so-called national emblem and the lettering "Deutschland erwache" ("Germany awake") mounted above the bronze door decorated with swastika patterns.[53] He also used similar elements for the memorial to the dead of Hitler's attempted putsch on 9 November 1923 which was mounted to the Feldherrnhalle in 1933. Troost even designed the brown dinner jackets worn by the members of the "National Socialist Reich Symphony Orchestra" during their performances.

According to the memoirs of Albert Speer published in 1966, Hitler's relationship to Troost was "something like that of an apprentice to a master". Furthermore, Speer talks of the positive influence exerted by Paul Ludwig Troost on Hitler's architectural taste: "It was as if 'scales had fallen from [my] eyes' when he saw the former's work. 'I couldn't bear any longer what I had drawn up to then. How lucky that I got to know this man'".[55] Gerdy Troost, who took a lively interest in her husband's duties, said virtually the same thing before the denazification court in 1947: "Hitler had told my husband that he had been attentively following him and his work, interior designs for steamers, for some time. It transpired that my husband and Hitler had the same artistic views [...] Hitler was enthusiastic about my husband and his opinions and he also explained to me on many occasions, even later when my husband was already dead, how greatly he admired and revered my husband, that he was the master of us all and that we could only learn from him. And so my husband was awarded various larger contracts [...] Hitler often came to us to discuss these plans. As far as I can remember, it was in early 1931 that I first met him. He was obsessed with architectural ideas [...] My husband also got the contracts for the party buildings at Königlicher Platz, for the Temples of Honour, and the House of German Art. All these plans had been completed by 1932. Later there were also smaller projects like redesigning the Physicians' House in Berlin and the Adolf Hitler House in Nuremberg."[56] Troost's appointment as architect of the NSDAP came at a time in which the rebuilding of the Lloyd fleet decimated by reparations was coming to an end. "I [...] am greatly called upon professionally, but not for interior work but exterior architectural work. Lloyd is currently not building any steamers and in my opinion it will be a long time until anyone starts thinking about building a new one in Bremen of a size that requires the involvement of architects," Paul Ludwig Troost reported to his brother in January 1932.[57] However, the new duties dominated not just his professional life. "We lived so intensely and consciously with each other in the realm of architecture, art and music. And, in turn, with each other for a higher ideal to which our entire life was dedicated over the last years," said Gerdy Troost looking back in 1934.[58] Paul Ludwig Troost had joined the NSDAP in August 1930[59] and now increasingly took an active part as an advocate of a militantly reactionary cultural policy. He was a member of the "Militant League for German Culture" formed under the leadership of Alfred Rosenberg in 1928 and the professional group of "German Architects and Engineers" founded in 1931/32 that had declared itself the enemy of all forms of functional modern building. In June 1933, he signed a sharply worded pronouncement "against the artistic pacemakers of the subversive communist revolution" and "personalities subversive to form such as Nolde, Schmitt-Rottluff, Klee, Mies van der Rohe".[60] As of April 1933, Troost was a member of Munich city council for the NSDAP and belonged to the advisory board for the municipal art collections. He resigned his seat on the city council after only a few months, however, justifying this step "with the great work overload from the assignment of a great task."[61] After the National Socialists had also come to power in Bavaria in March 1933 following a combination of putsch, violence and apparent legality, Troost was present in virtually all areas of life impacted by cultural policy. For example, the architect was even appointed judge of art and chairman of the jury for the "Munich Art Exhibition" that was displayed in the Neue Pinakothek in the Summer of 1933. "He will vigilantly ensure that Munich's reputation as a city of art does not fall any further but, on the contrary, will be raised again," was how his role was portrayed by Georg Steinlein in "Deutsche Bauzeitung".[62] How influential Troost had become in the meantime is demonstrated by the expulsion of Robert Vorhoelzer, the famous architect of post office buildings, from Munich Technical University in October 1933. Not only was the sculptor Karl Lösche, the real manipulator behind this campaign, promoted to the position of expert at the Ministry of Education and the Arts at the recommendation of Paul Ludwig Troost, but even the Minister of Education and the Arts, Hans Schemm, referred to the architect in a report as the highest instance, as it were, "after the Führer": Vorhoelzer bore the consequences of his post office buildings "that were described as being typically Bolshevistic". Troost also spoke "negatively of these buildings and therefore of Prof. Vorhoelzer".[63] In the meantime, Hitler's plans for the first representative buildings in the "Third Reich" had already started becoming concrete. Construction work on the "new administrative building" on Arcisstrasse commenced in September 1933; Hitler laid the foundation stone for the "House of German Art" in a pompous staged ceremony on 15 October. In addition to this, there was the extension work on Hitler's residential and working rooms in the Old Reich Chancery in Berlin. Paul Ludwig Troost did not live to see their completion. He died on 21 January 1934 following a brief but serious illness. Hitler ordered a state funeral for his late architect. SA and SS men stood vigil by the body. In an obituary in the "Münchner Neueste Nachrichten", Alexander Heilmeyer wrote, "Like Ludwig I. with regard to Master Builder Klenze, the Führer saw in Troost the man who was to design and implement his structural plans to continue the major Munich construction projects."[64] During the Nuremberg Party Rally in September 1937, the "German National Prize for Art and Science", newly created as the highest award in Nazi Germany, was awarded posthumously to Paul Ludwig Troost.[65] The honouring of Troost as the "Führer's First Builder" and "Arbitrator of German Architecture" had by this time become a permanent fixture of National Socialist cultural propaganda

First Class hall on the "Europa", 1926/30

and would not lose its validity until the collapse of the "Third Reich". In contrast, "Trooststrasse", a street running along Munich's Hofgarten, was given a much briefer lease of life. In eager compliance, Munich Mitte city council had resolved in October 1934 to rename Galeriestrasse after the "deceased Builder of the Führer".[66] But hardly had the new street sign been mounted, orders came from the highest authority to remove it again only a few weeks later. Hitler considered the street consisting of 38 house numbers to be too insignificant for his master builder. "A large square with the corresponding architectural arrangements will be created and the Führer intends to have Professor Troost honoured here and to name this square Troostplatz," was the proclamation made on 20 November 1934.[67] The project for which the area between Gabelsbergerstrasse and Alte Pinakothek had been earmarked never came to fruition, however.

2.2 The Troost Studio: Gerdy Troost and Leonhard Gall

According to Albert Speer, Hitler briefly toyed with the idea of carrying on Troost's office himself.[68] However, it was actually the architect's widow Gerdy Troost who took on management of the studio and, together with his long-standing employee, Leonhard Gall, completed the unfinished projects. Gerdy Troost was approaching her 30th birthday when she took on her husband's inheritance.[69] She had first met the architect in 1923 through her father Johannes Andresen. The manager of a Bremen-based wood art workshop and himself an interior architect had commercial links with Paul Ludwig Troost in connection with fitting out the interiors for the Norddeutscher Lloyd's steams; after finishing her schooling at the Higher Girls' School in Düsseldorf, his daughter also joined the handicraft business. Gerdy and Paul Ludwig Troost married in 1925. Six months previously, Gerdy Troost had arrived in Munich for "studies of architecture and art history". The young wife took great interest in her husband's work and became his closest advisor. In the same way as Paul Ludwig Troost, she was also, as she later stated, "impressed by Hitler"[70] and joined the NSDAP in 1932. Hitler's appreciation of her husband was transferred to her and it was to develop into a friendly relationship over the coming years. And so it was self-evident that Gerdy Troost was to continue her husband's work. "There was hardly a single thought of mine that I would not have shared with him," she wrote to a friend in December 1934. "At the Führer's request, all the buildings will be completed by Paulus here in the "Troost Studio (I gave the studio this name and have assumed management) [...] As there is no-one who can be as deeply empathetic to Paul Ludwig Troost's language & soul & to the spirit of his work as his employees and I. We feel, think & work completely in his spirit, whereas every other architect would, by nature, probably be able to adapt, but would ultimately speak his own language.[71] As Gerdy Troost did not have the requisite training and was likewise hardly qualified for such projects, she transferred technical management of the studio to Leonhard Gall, who had been employed in her husband's office since 1908.[72] Leonhard Gall, who had been a member of the NSDAP since 1932 like Gerdy Troost, produced the architectural plans and the draft drawings for the furnishings while Gerdy Troost primarily took on the task of representing the studio and ensured a correspondingly dignified arrangement using colour, material and décor. It was a matter of course that Gerdy Troost would also assess the furniture designs and their manufacture. With this constellation, the Troost Studio, which had as many as 19 employees at times and was one of the most highly remunerated firms in the "Third Reich", not only continued, as of 1934, the buildings at Königsplatz, the "House of German Art" and the work on the Old Reich Chancery in Berlin, but also, in Munich, designed the offices of the Lord Mayor in the Neues Rathaus, the official residence of the Minister of the Interior and Gauleiter Adolf Wagner in the Kaulbach Villa and the Prinz Carl Palais that was modified at the beginning of 1937 and was to serve as Mussolini's guest house on his state visits. In addition, the Troost Studio furnished Hitler's private flat at Prinzregentenplatz and the "Berghof" at Obersalzberg as elaborately as usual and exactly to the taste of the client. In 1939, Gerdy Troost assigned management of the studio to Leonhard Gall. Once the war had started, she shifted her professional focus to designing certificates for the awarding of the Iron Cross, which Nazi propaganda paid homage to as the highest decoration for bravery, and exquisite gifts for the Nazi leadership and their sympathizers.[73] As of this time, she also devoted herself intensely to expanding the "Archive and Work of Paul Ludwig Troost" for which, at Hitler's request, a building was to be built with a reproduction of the interior design of the Grand Hall of the Lloyd steamer "Europa".

For the rest of her life, Gerdy Troost saw herself as the trustee of a great inheritance that was faithfully tendered and continued by her – a role that National Socialist media coverage loved to attribute to her. As virtually the only woman, she was one of the actors on the Nazi

Gerdy Troost and Leonhard Gall (left) at the topping-out ceremony for the "House of German Art", 29 June 1935

art scene centering on the "House of German Art". Uncountable photographs and film reels taken between 1935 and 1944 on the occasion of pertinent events and festivities show her, to a certain extent in the role of "token woman", standing out from the uniformed mass as an elegant figure at the side of Adolf Hitler and high-ranking party members. "Dressed in a white suit, she sat in the first row for the guests of honour at ceremonies, she had a seat close to the Führer. After all, these celebratory days were at the same time days of honour for her. It was ultimately also her work that was being dedicated and handed over to the German people," reported the "Völkischer Beobachter" a few days after the inauguration of the "House of German Art."[74] Gerdy Troost enjoyed receiving the honours bestowed on the memory of her husband and herself. In 1937, Hitler awarded her the title of professor "in appreciation of an untiring, deep-seated willingness to keep watch that the legacy of her late husband is fulfilled to the last detail.[75] The same year, she was awarded the Grand Prix at the Paris World Exhibition for the "House of German Art" (a model of which was displayed on the "podium of honour" of the "German Building") and received the silver medal of honour from the Munich Academy of Fine Arts. She had already been appointed to the committee of the "House of German Art" in 1934. In Munich and party circles, Gerdy Troost was soon seen as "a kind of art judge".[76] How great Gerdy Troost's influence in the apparatus of power, dominated by intrigue and competition for authority, actually was cannot be clearly established using the sources available to date. With regard to Munich's cultural affairs at least, her judgement was decisive. Albert Speer whose rise began after Paul Ludwig Troost's death described her as "a woman of taste and character who was more persevering in the defence of her often idiosyncratic views as many a man in office and authority." She tackled colleagues who spoke critically of her husband's work, such as Paul Bonatz. Similarly, she had intervened vehemently against modern architects such as Adolf Abel or Robert Vorhoelzer and in doing so was, according to Speer, "of one opinion with Hitler in all these cases."[77]

Her good understanding with Hitler was surely one of the crucial factors in her appointment to the supervisory board of Bavaria Filmkunst GmbH in 1938, which was a constant competitor to Goebbels' protected UFA. "I assume that Professor Troost – now that she has a seat on Bavaria's supervisory board and the Führer sometimes has an ear for Mrs Troost in such concerns – will take the opportunity to present a few matters to the Führer", claimed a report by Erich Walter Herbell, Bavaria's general manager in which the paternalism from Berlin was brought up once again.[78] In addition, Gerdy Troost's name was frequently recommended for positions or the title of professor. The fact that her opinion also carried weight when it came to the so-called Aryanisation, i.e., the looting and deprivation of the rights of Jewish people, is evidenced at least in the case of Volkskunsthaus Wallach. At any event, party comrade and failed art dealer Otto Witte succeeded in acquiring the world-famous business for a knock-down price thanks to her intercession.[79] In contrast, Gerdy Troost, who had been awarded the "Golden Party Badge" in 1943[80] and remained an incorrigible adherent of Hitler to the very end, also used her influential position to assist colleagues, friends and acquaintances who were being persecuted or had fallen on hard times, a fact which she tried to use for her own ends after the end of the war based on dozens of affidavits. Like so many other intellectuals who had enjoyed a privileged status in the "Third Reich" and had promoted the Nazi tyranny with their activities, Gerdy Troost also laid claim to the much-cited cliché of the artist as a non-political figure. As an artist, her entire ambition had been directed solely towards architecture and the completion of her husband's work: "Open exclusively to the beautiful and bright things in life, she instinctively closed out the evil and dark things", asserted her lawyer in 1947 in his plea. "And so she only saw the bright sides of National Socialism in which she believed with a pure heart, incapable of suspecting disguise and deceit."[81] Although the lawyers succeeded in protracting the court proceedings until March 1950, the denazification court classified her as a "lesser offender". As a beneficiary and convinced supporter of the National Socialist tyranny, she was sentenced to pay a financial reparation and was deprived of her civil and personal rights for a two-year probationary period. The entitlement to use her professional title was withdrawn because "no independent artistic work of exceptional value had ever been performed by her that would have justified the awarding of the title at that time."[82] Gerdy Troost lived in seclusion in Bad Reichenhall in Upper Bavaria until her death on 30 January 2003.

Leonhard Gall was also rewarded for his services with numerous offices and awards. As vice-president of the Reich Chamber of Fine Arts and member of the artistic advisory board of the City of Munich and having been appointed professor in 1935 on the occasion of the roofing ceremony for the "House of German Art", he was primarily active at the level of cultural policy. In 1936, Joseph Goebbels appointed him trustee of the "Künstlerdank" endowment donated by the Propaganda Ministry, a kind of welfare fund for artists approved by the regime who were in need of support. In addition, Leonhard Gall was an editor – alongside Albert Speer and the sculptor Richard Klein – of the authoritative journal "Die Kunst im Dritten Reich" (from 1939 onwards "Die Kunst im Deutschen Reich") which had been published by the party's own publishing house since January 1937 and brought the National Socialist notion of art into German homes with a print run of up to 50,000 copies. During the Second World War, Gall was one of the "irreplaceable artists" who, exempted from military service and provided with unlimited privileges, did not have to fear any obstruction to their work.[83] Despite these honours, Leonhard Gall was completely overshadowed as an architect by his deceased "master teacher", Paul Ludwig Troost. Even as late as in 1944 on the occasion of his 60th birthday, the contemporary press dubbed him the "innovative guardian of a great legacy" who was able to look back with the knowledge of "having [...] worked together as a close associate of Paul Ludwig Troost on the development of the architectural style of our time."[84] Apart from one-off monumental projects such as the "House of German Architecture" on Prinzregentenstrasse and an NSDAP chancery building opposite the Alte Pinakothek, Leonard Gall played only a marginal role in the "restructuring of the Capital of the Movement" planned from 1938/39. After 1945, a large number of witnesses for the defence, mainly recruited from Munich's artists and architects attested his untiring commitment to his artistic work that "did not permit any political use."[85] Finally in November 1948, the exceedingly lenient denazification court classified the architect as a "follower" and found a remarkable explanation even for his rapidly increasing income in the "massive upswing in construction activities in the Third Reich." Not least because of his age, Leonhard Gall no longer succeeded in gaining a foothold as an architect in the bustling reconstruction phase of the post-war years. He occupied himself from then on with unsuccessful furniture designs. An illuminated sign in the form of a gateway was probably the only project implemented in this period; it was designed in 1949 for the east wing of the "House of German Art" (that had been renamed "Haus der Kunst" – "House of Art") and remained in use until 1957 as a billboard among other things. Aged 68, Leonhard Gall died in Munich on 20 January 1952.

Gerdy Troost surrounded by Nazi celebrities: Opening tour of the "Great German Art Exhibition", 1939. On the right, Karl Kolb, director of the "House of German Art"

View of the Hofgarten area, Von-der-Tann-Strasse and Prinzregentenstrasse, 1937

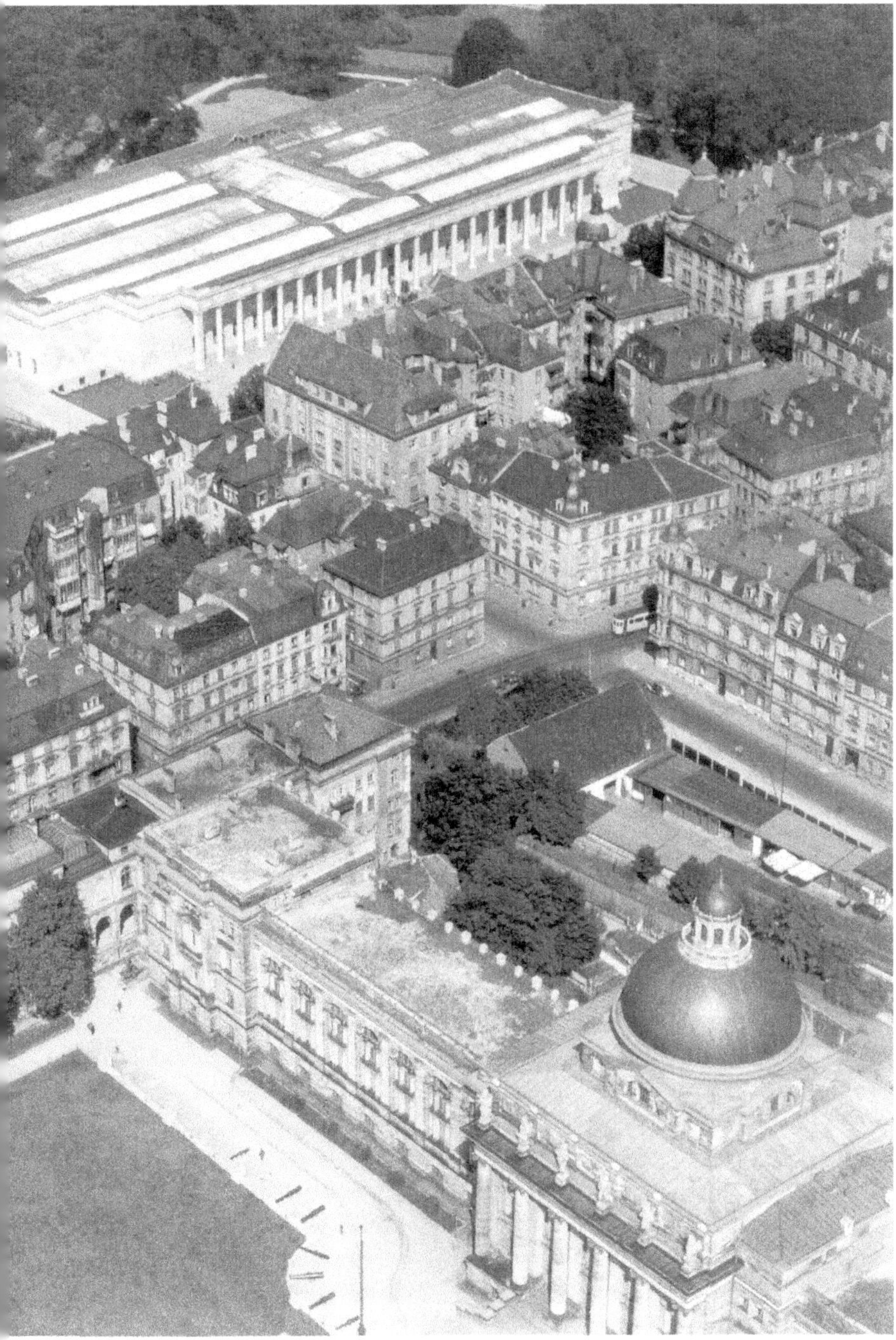

3 The "House of German Art"

3.1 The surrounding urban development

Hitler had not only determined who was going to be the architect of the "House of German Art" but he interfered radically in the choice of location. "And now it is quite definite," reported the well-informed journal "Bauzeitung" on 5 May 1933, "that the place in the Old Botanical Gardens will be left behind; they want to retain it as a place for popular recreation at the heart of the city. There are prospects that a part of the Englischer Garten on the inner Prinzregentenstrasse will become available as a new construction site."[86] The area at the southern end of the Englischer Garten had been under discussion once before as a location for an art exhibition building. In 1823, Johann Georg von Dillis, the then director of the royal picture galleries, had made a recommendation to the crown prince and later King Ludwig I to build the New Gallery there – today's Alte Pinakothek. Besides, the site had become increasingly attractive through the construction of the Prinzregentenstrasse in 1891, which had developed into a residential area favoured by the upper middle classes and had consequently become a gold mine for estate agents and speculators. The concept, popular in itself, of adding a third exhibition building (alongside the Bavarian National Museum and the Schack Galerie) to Prinzregentenstrasse and freeing up the site of the Old Botanical Gardens as a "green lung" at the centre of the inner city[87] probably played, at the very most, a secondary role in Hitler's thinking. Rather, he imagined a monumental forum stretching deep into the Englischer Garten (and for which the Old Botanical Garden would not have offered sufficient space). In addition to the "House of German Art", the concept involved a "Museum of Contemporary History" and a palace for the Reich governor. The forum plan was scuppered by resistance on the part of Paul Ludwig Troost who is said to have vehemently campaigned for the preservation of the Englischer Garten and otherwise threatened to resign from his commission.[88] The decision to build the "House of German Art" as a solitary building at the edge of the Englischer Garten did, however, encounter critical opinions – even if they were only isolated and expressed with the necessary caution. In the Munich city council it was the Bayerische Volkspartei fraction that made up its mind to make a statement – before they were forced out of the city hall on July 1933 by the National Socialists. They feared "that the Englischer Garten may suffer damage from such a design."[89] Similar misgivings were also held by music historian Bertha Antonia Walln, a resident of the quarter, who stood up as a lone fighter advocating the preservation of the Englischer Garten: "Very much in the interest of art and artists, a replacement of the Glass Palace must be welcomed, it is equally deplorable if one of the most magnificent centrally located landscapes is destroyed by building development. At the same time, there is an increasing danger that the Englischer Garten overall will slowly develop into building plots," she wrote to "Bayerische Gartenbau-Gesellschaft" on 12 May 1933, without failing to point out that there was "absolutely no party political intent" in her letter.[90] As was unambiguously worded in a memorandum of the Bavarian Administration of Palaces, Gardens and Lakes, the following applied to this and any other objections: "The plans relating to the House of German Art have been drafted by the architect in permanent consultation with the Reich Chancellor and have been approved by him. The choice of the building site was also the latter's wish. Any statements on the details of the project seem out of place under such circumstances."[91] Discussions on the other urban development measures and plans associated with the building of the "House of German Art" were likewise fully out the question. In this respect, the highest priority was given to the widening, ordered by Hitler in person, of Von-der-Tann-Strasse as the "main access road to the House of German Art" and the representative link between Prinzregentenstrasse and Ludwigsstrasse in the direction of Königsplatz. It should not go unmentioned in this context that the area along the Ludwigstrasse and Von-der-Tann-Strasse was intended to be used for redevelopment of the Hofgarten in which Hitler briefly considered having a monumental opera house built. Demolition of the buildings along the southern side began in February 1937 after their owners had consented to a sale mostly much lower than the asking price, following a threat of expropriation.[92] In the course of the road construction work, the annexe of Prinz-Carl-Palais that housed the supreme court of auditors was demolished and the surviving palace was correspondingly rebuilt according to plans by Fritz Gablonsky the head of the structural engineering department of the Ministry of the Interior.[93] But it was not just the southern side of Von-der-Tann-Strasse which was affected by the new structural activities. The Nazi rulers felt the renowned Art Nouveau façade of the former "Elvira" photographic studio on the northern side of the road to be an "irritating foreign body". This unique ornament, designed by August Endell in 1898, took the form of a coloured dragon, and had to be removed at the orders of the Ministry of the Interior. The owner received an express letter on 1 July 1937 containing instructions from the local building commission of the "Capital of the Movement" to take measures within ten days to "change the ugly façade that greatly disturbs the appearance of the street [...] in such a way that the existing ornaments are removed and replaced by flat wall plastering and a new coat of paint."[94]

A further monumental building was added to Prinzregentenstrasse in 1938 in the form of an imposing complex of buildings adorned with martial façade elements from the district air command (today's Ministry of Economics), standing opposite the National Museum. The same year, Hitler gave orders for the construction of the "House of German Architecture", an exhibition building for architectural and artistic trades that was designed by Leonhard Gall and was to be located opposite the "House of German Art". With this, the plans were for Prinzregentenstrasse to be finally developed into a magnificent stone avenue and, to a certain extent to become a counterpart to the political alignment of Königsplatz, as a "via triumphalis of the arts" that captivated individuals and masses alike. As was already the case with the "House of German Art", the intention was for the private sector to provide most of the financing. Already in April 1939, August von Finck, who exercised his connections in the usual manner, was able to report to the "Führer" on his 50th birthday that "the financing of the building costs for the second exhibition building [had] been secured within the estimated figures."[95] By this time, the city of Munich had declared its readiness to provide the building land required for the project at the near end of Prinzregentenstrasse along with the pertinent side streets although the properties were still privately owned at this point. From now on, it was a matter of inducing the owners to sell their property – but the threat of forced expropriation proceedings did not fail to have an effect. On the other hand, the owners were offered Jewish properties; for example, the owners of the property at Pilotystrasse 4 let the City of Munich have their house subject to the condition that the authorities obtained the "Jews' property at Mozartstrasse 12" for them in return.[96] Decisive assistance in this respect was provided by the company "Vermögensverwertung München GmbH", the vehicle used by Gauleiter and the Minister of the Interior Adolf Wagner since Kristallnacht in November 1938 in order to employ dramatic means to "Aryanise" Jewish assets and property. For instance, the company also exerted the necessary pressure on Jutta Oppenheimer, the owner of Mozartstrasse 12, to move her to sell her property for the taxable value of 63,000 Reichsmarks – a price that had been expressly set too low. Jutta Oppenheimer succeeded in fleeing to the US in 1940, thus avoiding imminent deportation. The "Aryan" tenants in the buildings scheduled to be demolished to make way for the planned "House of German Architecture" were compensated at the cost of Munich's Jewish citizens. Even before the law was passed in 1939 annulling tenancy protection for Jews and Jewish tenants were driven out of their flats and were forcibly re-quartered, Munich's Lord Mayor Fiehler had 250 flats cleared with immediate effect and obtained a special regulation providing unlimited rights of securing Jewish homes which had become vacant in the course of persecution.[97] Like most of the Nazis' major construction projects, the "House of German Architecture" was never built.

The "House of German Art" and the building intended to supplement it, the "House of German Architecture". Painting by Otto A. Hirth, displayed at the "Great German Art Exhibition", 1940

3.2. Design and implementation

The "House of German Art" was the first monumental building that the National Socialist rulers aired in public. This "new home of German art" was unanimously hailed as the symbol immortalised in stone of the "power of the National Socialist German Reich" and "the will to create new culture and art."[98] Munich's press had been extensively presenting maps and ground plans of the planned exhibition building to the general public since July 1933. In addition, there was, as of 22 July, an opportunity to view the model of the "House of German Art" in the round temple in Munich's Hofgarten. As the "Münchner Neueste Nachrichten" reported, "this was in accordance with the Führer's special wishes, who wants the entire German people to share in these great plans that give Munich new prestige and greater significance as a city of art."[99] In a similar vein, Hitler gave orders that SA men should stand guard day and night before the model on display, which was interpreted as a "sign of the general, public significance the Führer attributes to art in German life."[100] Hardly four months later the "Völkischer Beobachter" and the "Münchner Neueste Nachrichten" announced the beginning of construction work on the southern edge of the Englischer Garten, emphasising that the major project provided job creation schemes for hundreds of unemployed people.[101] Many Munich and Germany based workshops, industrial businesses and commercial enterprises had also clearly taken note of the reports in the press. They offered their services in countless letters that have survived in the inventory of the Haus der Kunst's historical archive. In light of the generally compliant atmosphere and a decree already issued by Lord Mayor Fiehler on 24 March 1933 that no municipal orders would be placed with non-German firms,[102] only very few missed the opportunity to point out their "Aryan" convictions. Thus, a firm based in Aschaffenburg affirmed its "application for orders for bronze structures" in the following way: "owner and general managers of our firm can prove their Aryan ancestry. No Jewish capital is utilized in the business; similarly, no Jewish workers or clerks are employed. When purchasing raw material, we also carefully pay attention that only Christian suppliers are used."[103] The owner of a Munich tinsmith's shop placed all his bets on his commitment to National Socialism and went into great detail to describe how he had put his offices and private quarters at the disposal of the party's own defence and press office "completely voluntarily and for no cost" during Hitler's trial in 1924. He likewise did not forget to comment on the fact that "at that time Jewish tenants [...] made every effort to make things impossible [for him] in town, both commercially and personally, on account of his support for the national cause."[104] Very often representatives of the Nazi leadership interceded on behalf of deserving old party comrades to facilitate the awarding of contracts. For example, the adjutant of the Gauleiter and Minister of the Interior Adolf Wagner promoted the Munich master painter and "holder of the badge of honour" Josef Rauwolf.[105] Was the status of "Old Fighter of the Movement" ultimately decisive in awarding an order? A 1939 list of all firms involved in the construction and the interior fittings of the "House of German Art" reveals that this assumption only applied in some individual cases.[106] The Troost architectural office mainly gave preference to businesses based in Munich that they had already successfully worked together with for many years. Thus, Vereinigte Werkstätten produced a large portion of the furnishings according to Leonhard Gall's plans. Nevertheless, various firms included in the directory had close commercial links to the party. As an example, the construction firm Leonhard Moll quoted that, as was still stated in the company history in 1969, it was ready "for the major construction tasks of the following years in which state-sponsored measures brought in significant orders."[107] Moll not only took care of the demolition of Munich's main synagogue ordered by Hitler in 1938 but, as of 1942, also profited from the exploitation of forced labourers and concentration camp prisoners who were deployed for the construction of underground aircraft plants. Philipp Holzmann AG was also involved in this inhumane undertaking. In November 1933, this firm had been awarded the contract for the excavation and foundation work for the "House of German Art". On account of the poor ground conditions, it was necessary to put in a pile foundation involving 1,180 reinforced concrete piles that bound together to form a supporting structure and were used to compact the foundation soil. As little as eleven months later, the foundation walls were built. At this point, 340 workers from Leonhard Moll were employed on the large-scale construction site. The "first piece of Third Reich culture to become visible" had been completed after a total of 45 months. While materials were deployed such as steel, iron and concrete, which were ostracised when used by modernism, they did however remain out of sight. For example, the steel frame construction of the exhibition halls was faced with a monumental architectural covering of Danube limestone, that served

Construction site of the "House of German Art" on 5 September 1934 (above) and on 26 March 1935

as the building material for the entire superstructure and the pillared halls along the northern and southern façades, while the substructure and the terraces were made of gompholite "in order to create a harmonious transition to the park landscape."[108]

Troost's plans for the "House of German Art" date back to drafts he conceived in 1931 in connection with the competition for the reconstruction of the Glass Palace but had not submitted "because he", as was later maintained, "anticipated that they would not be understood in light of the attitudes prevailing at that time."[109] Even these initial plans reveal that they were directly modelled on Schinkel's Museum am Lustgarten built in 1825/1829. The revival of the classicistic model is characterised, however, by a monumentalisation and oversimplification that is directly linked to the pretension to power asserted by the National Socialist regime and was propagated by the press (in line with official policy) as "an architectural style arising from a new German attitude to life."[110] With this, the architect and principal set the standards for a National Socialist representative architecture that, after Paul Ludwig Troost's death, was to intensify into a construction ideology dominated by gigantomania and a ruling principle of totalitarianism. The change from the row of pillars intended by Troost to a columned colonnade may even have stemmed from Hitler himself.[111] This intervention in the design of the façade gave much greater clarity to the latter's demands for a "temple of art" – as the building was generally described with regard to its purpose.[112] "The regular structure of this Doric order," praised Alexander Heilmeyer 1937 "has the same effect on the eye as ceremonial music has on the ear. If one thinks, in this context, of people in a festive mood, passing up the steps and being received by this choir of columns, being prepared for a dignified entry into the temple of art, then one also understands the actual purpose of the building that, contrary to a private dwelling, is intended to lead day-to-day life into the realm of arts and ideals."[113] If one contemplates contemporary photographs depicting uniformed formations and parades with standards in the colonnade of the "House of German Art", the people standing in rank and file seem to merge with the building. Mass and architecture form the backdrop for the ceremonies stage by the Nazi rulers. Correspondingly, the building with a length of 155 metres and a width of 55 metres was intentionally left unadorned.[114] A colourful meandering mosaic on the panelled ceiling of the colonnades and three bronze reliefs (removed after 1945) over the portals on Prinzregentenstrasse were the only, but very mean-

Bronze reliefs on the southern facade of the "House of German Art", photograph taken in 1937

ingful, decorative elements. And so the main entrance was adorned by a "national eagle" designed by Kurt Schmidt-Ehmen (who produced party emblems for virtually all public buildings); quotations from Hitler's cultural policy speeches were mounted over the side entrances – a clear signal as to whose dictum the fine arts would have to follow in future. The interior of the building was similarly geared to the needs of self-presentation and monumentality. Strict symmetry dominated here, too. Dark red and light yellow marble are to this day the defining factors in the rooms' appearance. Going through the main entrance, you first reach a vestibule where the ticket office and cloakroom are located. Two "plaques of honour" (removed after 1945) were also positioned here in memory of the "donors of the foundation stone"[115] and the architect of the building. Wide corridors with administrative rooms and sanitary facilities branch off from both sides of this foyer. The centre point of the building is formed by the so-called "Hall of Honour" (today: Central Hall), a sky-lit hall separated into three aisles by pillars, around which all rooms are grouped in a strict arrangement. In accordance with its intended purpose as representative reception hall, the plinths, walls and pillars were edged with blood red Tegernsee marble. The omnipresence of the colour red, which is the dominant colour of the NSDAP's swastika flag, should conjure up the omnipresence of National Socialist ideology. While Paul Ludwig Troost had intended the Hall of Honour to be used for exhibiting large sculptures and holding festivities for artists, it was used between 1937 and 1944 exclusively for the opening of exhibitions and press conferences. In order to create an effective stage, despite the poor acoustics, for speeches by Hitler and other Nazi bigwigs, the side aisles of the 11 metres high and 35 metres long hall were fitted out with specially produced chandeliers containing built-in loudspeakers. Similarly, Prinzregentenstrasse could be filled with sound from mushroom-shaped loudspeakers along the entire length of the building. A permanently installed microphone system additionally ensured that the entire German people could share in the speeches and ceremonies through the radio – according to Joseph Goebbels the "most modern and [...] most important instrument of mass influence [...] of all."[116] A total of 24 classically designed gallery rooms adjoin the Hall of Honour to the right and the left; the arrangement of these rooms – in each case, a 39 metre by 14 metre central room surrounded by eleven smaller rooms – created a ground plan of greatest regularity. The mighty semi-spheres of the fillets that connected the walls whitewashed in broken white with the skylights facilitated plastic modelling

Opening speech by Adolf Hitler held in the "Hall of Honour" on 18 July 1937

Bar, photograph taken in 1938

of the rooms with light. A mid-height plinth made of yellow Jurassic marble, running around the walls, not only gave the rooms their imposing character – it ultimately determined the way in which the paintings exhibited there were presented; they always had to be hung at the same distance from the upper edge of the marble cladding. In addition, the rubber carpets laid throughout the entire building created a visible guideline that showed visitors the prescribed way through the exhibition and did not permit any individual decisions. While the big rooms were determined for monumental paintings and sculptures, the upper storey, accessed by stone staircases at the four corners of the building, offered space for graphic art and craftwork. The middle section of these narrower, elongated rooms rose over the front sides of the Hall of Honour where they appeared as open galleries; A spatial solution that Paul Ludwig Troost and Leonhard Gall had taken on from international museum architecture. The gastronomical facilities were on the side towards the Englischer Garten Today's "Goldene Bar", in which a dance band played during the Nazi period, was one of the hospitality facilities that were open the whole year round, just like the spacious café-restaurant and the "Bierstüberl" pub in the western basement floor of the building. This meant that the "sublime artistic experience" that the "Great German Art Exhibitions" had to convey to the people could be combined with gastronomical pleasures. The terrace used for restaurant service was very popular, especially on warm summer days. In order to be able to cherish delightful views "of beautiful trees, green park areas and the Monopteros,"[117] Adolf Hitler had personally given the order in 1936 to fell the groups of trees at the northern side "in the very near future".[118] Based on Gerdy Troost's ideas, the interior design of the bar was implemented by Munich architect Ernst Haiger who also redesigned the German Venice Biennale pavilion in 1938. The golden mural was the work of Karl-Heinz Dallinger, who was already an acquaintance of the Troosts since the 20s and whose career had begun with paintings on farmhouses.[119] Its topic, a geography of international cuisine and cultural history of fine drinks, may be surprising at first glance. But specifically the suggestion of an international flair was an essential element of Nazi propaganda and was intended to make a contribution to strengthening the national self-confidence of "fellow Germans" and to present to other countries an impression of the cosmopolitanism of German visions. It was, however, not only propaganda elements that made up the staged appearance of the exhibition building. Some of the most modern and progressive technical equipment was hidden behind the stone monumentality. The building had three lifts, a state-of-the-art lighting system and a combined heating and air conditioning system that – in addition to the two staff apartments, various workshops, storage rooms and an air raid shelter for 300 persons – was located in the basement of the building and was proudly designated the "technical heart of the building."[120] At the same time, the shining measuring instruments and control equipment, the enamelled wide-beam lamps beneath the roof and – still visible for every visitor today – the door handles and fittings in the administrative rooms and sanitary facilities are, in their design, reminiscent of the language of modernism and Bauhaus so hated at that time. This juxtaposition of apparent extremes of traditionalism, technology and functional aesthetics marks the "House of German Art" as architecture that, as art historian Dieter Bartetzko remarks in an essay on the architects of the "Third Reich" published in 2004, "appeared equally dynamic and persistent, modern and timeless and thus corresponded in an ideal way to the architectural concepts of the Nazis who wanted to see in their buildings stone guarantees of the absurd assertion that the "Third Reich" was modern and conservative at the same time, was committed to eternal values but still ahead of its time."[121]

3.3 Financing

The construction of the "House of German Art" required a total of nine million Reichsmarks. Considering the considerable financing problems which Adolf Abel's – far cheaper – project had already fought with, the question arises as to how this vast amount was raised within such a short period of time. The driving force turned out to be Gauleiter Adolf Wagner, who had held the office of Bavarian Minister of the Interior since March 1933. "The man with the bald, energetic skull", who was seen to be the "definitive initiator behind bringing Bavaria in line with the Nazi party line" and was among Hitler's closest associates, soon advanced to a virtually all-powerful authority and was to also take on the cultural matters of Munich "City of Art" in his usual imperious manner.[122] Only a few days after the National Socialists had come to power in Bavaria he had already taken the initiative to press forward with the financing of the new building. Wealthy sponsors were needed for the construction project that was estimated to cost five million Reichsmarks at that point – and without the patronage of German business and industry it would hardly have been possible to implement the project. First, Wagner informed Friedrich Doehlemann, the director of Bayerische Gemeindebank, of the "Führer's pet idea" of building a representative exhibition building for fine arts in Munich. Doehlemann, who also campaigned for the Winter Olympic Games in 1936, soon declared his willingness to take on the matter and by mid-April he was able to present "a letter with the signatures of six public associations, companies and institutions" in which the signatories held out the prospect of a total of 125,000 Reichsmarks.[123] This marked the beginning of a successful fundraising campaign. On 31 May, Adolf Wagner invited "around twelve gentlemen from all over Germany" to a meeting which, as he put it a few days later in a letter to Reich governor Ritter von Epp represented "on the whole, representatives of high finance". Those present announced unanimously "that it would be no problem to organise the amount," Wagner further reported, "namely in the form of donations none of which individually will be any less than 25,000 Reichsmarks. The work is intended to be a gift for the Führer who in the time of Germany's greatest need took the burden of responsibility on himself."[124] Mid-June 1933, the government under Prime Minister Ludwig Siebert founded a public institution that bore the name "Haus der Deutschen Kunst (Neuer Glaspalast)" ["House of German Art (New Glass Palace)"] – the addendum in brackets was to be understood as a reminder of the destroyed Glass Palace; it was presumably this tradition that many a donor also wished their financial commitment to be connected to.[125] The statute passed on 14th July was based mainly on proposals by Dr. Max Grasmann, the managing director of the Bavarian Industrial Association. Reportedly, the institution was responsible for the erection and administration of an art exhibition building; furthermore, its duties included "bringing together friends and opening up ways and means of supporting the work of visual artists and of securing the position of German art in Germany and abroad", which included in particular the holding of exhibitions.[126] According to section three of the statute, the exhibition was dedicated to Adolf Hitler, who also acted as patron. The institution was subject to supervision by the Bavarian state; Adolf Wagner was appointed state commissioner to perform this duty. In addition, the following belonged to the honorary committee during their tenures: Reich governor Ritter von Epp, the Bavarian Prime Minister Ludwig Siebert, the Bavarian Minister of Justice and later "Governor General" of Poland Hans Frank, Lord

Mayor of Munich Karl Fiehler, along with Joseph Goebbels and Hermann Goering, the latter in his capacity as Prussian Prime Minister. Any person who had been of great service to the institution and therefore to German artistic life could be nominated as honorary members by the committee. Munich banker August von Finck had been appointed chairman of the institution by Adolf Hitler; this office opened useful connections to the Nazi leadership up to him and, according to his own statement, he had at that time "been travelling for more than fifty nights in order to raise the necessary funds for the construction work from his circles of friends in industry and commerce.[127] Friedrich Doehlemann acted as treasurer. The committee and board were mainly comprised of leading representatives of German business and industry, such as Wilhelm Kißkalt, the general director of Münchener Rückversicherungsgesellschaft; Albert Pietzsch, the president of the chamber of industry and commerce in Munich; Wilhelm von Opel; Karl Friedrich von Siemens and Fritz Thyssen as well as the general director of the Bavarian State Painting Collections, Dr. Ernst Buchner; Paul Ludwig Troost and Reich treasurer Franz Xaver Schwarz. In order to boost donation generosity, Hitler had pushed through tax exemption for foundations of over 25,000 Reichsmarks against the resistance of the finance minister.[128] But it was not only prominent German business people who were called upon to sponsor the construction of the "House of German Art". From mid-July 1933, the press, which toed the party line, appealed to the "entire German people" to make as a gift to "the Führer the fulfilment of this, his favourite wish."[129] By the time the building was completed in July 1937, more than ten million Reichsmarks of donations in money and in kind had been collected.[130] It was, of course, not possible to completely dispense with public funds. In 1934, the 33,000 square metre plot of land at the southern edge of the Englischer Garten valued at 1,778,000 Reichsmarks was transferred from the ownership of the Bavarian state to that of the institution "House of German Art (New Glass Palace)" as a "donation of a building site". The law passed on 27 December 1933 on the gratuitous transfer of a state-owned plot of land for the construction of the "House of German Art" provided the legal basis for this transaction.[131] Moreover, Prime Minister Ludwig Siebert granted a government subsidy of 500,000 Reichsmarks "on the one hand, to express thanks to the Führer for the promotion of this building of such great importance to Bavaria and, on the other, to demonstrate his interest in the Bavarian capital and for Bavarian art and provision of further opportunities for work."[132] His suggestion of designating a place in the completed building for a statue of Adolf Hitler was not taken up, however. The City of Munich donated 400,000 Reichsmarks from the "fund for the acquisition of works of fine art."[133] In addition, the institution had been able to obtain an interest-free loan worth one and half million Reichsmarks from the "Deutsche Gesellschaft für öffentliche Arbeit" ("German Society for Public Works") by declaring the construction project as a "special case" with reference to the "Führer's will" thus making it possible to circumvent the requirements prescribed.[134] The donations organised by the Bavarian Industrial Association were also considerable. For example, the Bavarian electricity works provided free supplies of electricity for the duration of 30 years,[135] Deutsche Reichsbahn provided free shipping for all construction materials and machines required for the construction work. The construction was mainly financed with the cash donations of German industrialists as well as individual companies, banks, savings banks and breweries. The NSDAP donated a mere 200,000 Reichsmarks. The "foundation stone donation" initiated by August von Finck was of special significance, bringing in two million Reichsmarks alone from 18 donors and two foundations[136] and enabling the foundation works to be carried out as planned. In 1934, the board of the "House of German Art" had already decided to "erect a memorial to the willingness of these men to make sacrifices": their names were to be immortalised on a "plaque of honour".[137] The bronze plaque designed by Josef Wackerle ultimately hung in the foyer of the building from 1937 onwards and was removed after 1945. After being stored for decades in the cellar of the building (today's historical archive) it has been on public display again since 2003. The plaque, the names on which to this day read like a who's who of German business and industry, is not just a conspicuous document on the history of the building. Nevertheless, it represents the question of how deeply the persons listed there were involved in the structures of power and vested interests of National Socialism. This chapter should therefore come to a conclusion with a look at the lives of the "foundation stone donors".[138]

Robert Bosch

born in Albeck near Ulm in 1861, died in Stuttgart in 1942

Robert Bosch's rise to become a major German industrialist began in 1886 with the opening of a "workshop for precision mechanics and electrical engineering". Through technical innovations for vehicles, the workshop facilities that started off on a small scale developed into a profitable business around the turn of the century that in the 1920s Robert Bosch expanded into an internationally operating electrical engineering group. In 1906, Bosch was one of the first business owners in Germany to introduce the eight-hour day. In addition, he founded several generous foundations for charitable purposes. He was a member of various business organisations, an honorary professor at the Technical College in Stuttgart and belonged to the committee of the "House of German Art." On the occasion of his 80th birthday and the 55th anniversary of the founding of the Bosch Works, Adolf Hitler presented him with the "Pioneer of Labour" award. He received a state funeral in 1942.

August Diehn

born in Ribnitz, Mecklenburg, in 1874, died in Berlin in 1942

August Diehn, who presided over a trading company in Indonesia (at that time, Dutch East Indes) during the First World War, was the general director and board member of Deutsche Kalisyndikat GmbH in 1925; potash mining operations had been combined into the business since 1919. As a member of the "circle of economic leaders", August Diehn acted as an advisor to Joseph Goebbels in questions of Germany's international propaganda. He had promised Hitler his financial support as early as 1931. Diehn held numerous honorary posts and sat on the committee of the "House of German Art".

Theodor Feise

born in Hanover in 1871, died in Sehnde near Hanover in 1946.

Since 1911 director and from 1926 onwards general director of Kaliwerke Friedrichshall AG, Theodor Feise was one of the most important people in the German potash industry. Theodor Feise belonged to the honorary committee of the "House of German Art", was a member of the German Academy for German Law and was a "war industry leader". After the end of the Second World War he had to resign from his offices.

August von Finck

born in Kochel am See in 1898, died in Möschenfeld in 1980

August von Finck was the son of Wilhelm von Finck (1848–1924), the founder of the private bank Merck, Finck & Co. and co-founder of the Münchener Rückversicherung and Allianz-Versicherungs AG insurance companies. After his father's death in 1924, August von

Finck and his two sisters, baroness Margarethe von Stengel and Elisabeth Winterstein, became shareholders in the bank and joined the supervisory board of numerous industrial enterprises. For example, he was chairman of the supervisory board of Allianz-Stuttgarter Verein Versicherungs AG (Bayerische Versicherungsbank AG), Münchener Rückversicherungs-Gesellschaft, Aktienbrauerei zum Löwenbräu in Munich, Isarwerke AG in Munich and Süddeutschen Bodencreditbank and sat on numerous expert panels. In 1933, he was a member of the General Council for the Economy, the senate of the German Academy and was the chairman of the board of the institution "House of German Art" in Munich. Finck, who had joined the NSDAP in 1933, used his distinguished name to make important connections for Hitler. Following the annexation of Austria in 1938 he profited from the "Aryanisation" of Jewish banks and took over Rothschild-Bank and Bankhaus J. Dreyfus & Co. in Vienna. August von Finck was dismissed from his offices and the bank on the grounds of denazification terms, and the bank was administered by a trustee. Classified as a "follower" in 1948, Finck had become deputy chairman of the supervisory board of Münchener Rückversicherungs-Gesellschaft again by 1951.

Wilhelm von Finck – Memorial Foundation

The Wilhelm von Finck Gedächtnisstiftung (Memorial Foundation) was founded by Elisabeth Winterstein, née von Finck, in memory of her older brother, Wilhelm. Wilhelm von Finck was killed in the Battle of Verdun in 1916, aged 26. Elisabeth Winterstein donated 100,000 Reichsmarks from the Wilhelm von Finck Memorial Foundation for the construction of the "House of German Art".

Friedrich Flick

born in Ernsdorf-Kreuztal in 1883, died in Constance in 1972

As founder of the steel works company, Mitteldeutsche Stahlwerke, Friedrich Flick was one of the most powerful industrialists of the Weimar Republic. Growing up in modest circumstances, he had built up one of the largest metal conglomerates in Germany through his skill in negotiating business purchases and at the beginning of the 1920s had gained a foothold in the coal and steel industry. In the Nazi period, Flick profited from his good National Socialist leadership contacts, who received from him a total of 7.65 million Reichmarks in donations. He was a paid member of "Himmler's Circle of Friends" and was awarded the title of “war industry leader” in 1937. Shortly before this, he had entered the NSDAP. Since 1933 he was a member of the honorary committee of the “House of German Art”. During the Second World War he advanced to become the largest armaments supplier of the Nazi regime, making him an accessory to their policy of annihilation. Some 50,000 slave labourers and inmates from concentration camps were forcibly conscripted to work in his factories under the most inhumane conditions. In 1947, the Nuremberg Tribunal sentenced him to seven years imprisonment as a war criminal from which he was granted early released in 1950. Flick was able to rebuild his empire over the following years. When he died in 1972, he was thought to be the richest man in Germany.[139]

Adolf Haeuser

born in Weilburg an der Lahn in 1857, died in Frankfurt am Main in 1938

He graduated in law and chemistry and whilst founding I. G. Farbenindustrie, at that time the largest chemical company in Germany, he first became a member of the supervisory board and in 1926 the deputy chairman of the administrative board. He retired in 1932. Adolf Haeuser held numerous offices in cultural and scientific associations. He was, for example, a member of the board of the Deutsches Museum in Munich and belonged to the honorary committee of the “House of German Art”.

Johann Jakob Haßlacher

born in Saarbrücken in 1869, died in Schwarzach-St. Veit near Gastein in 1940

As general director from 1910 onwards, Johann Jakob Haßlacher controlled the fate of Rheinische Stahlwerke in Duisburg-Ruhrort, which merged with other companies in 1926 to become the largest coal and steel conglomerate in Europe, “Vereinigte Stahlwerke”. Holding a doctorate in law, he was an election candidate for the Reichstag in 1928 as a member of the Deutschnationale Volkspartei and was a town councillor in Duisburg. He was, among other things, a member of Ruhrort’s Chamber of Commerce, the board of the Reich Association of German Industry and, as of 1933, sat on the honorary committee of the “House of German Art”.

Plaque honouring the "donors of foundation stones" for the "House of German Art", photograph taken in 2004

Gustav Krupp von Bohlen und Halbach

born in The Hague in 1870, died in Blühnbach Castle near Salzburg

Through his marriage to the Krupp daughter Bertha, Gustav von Bohlen und Halbach, who up to then had been in diplomatic service, joined the supervisory board of the Krupp Works in 1906 and four years later assumed management of the company that belonged to the largest heavy industry businesses in the world. In 1943, Hitler personally decreed in a special regulation, the "Lex Krupp", for the stock company to be transformed into a family-owned business. As early as in 1933, Gustav Krupp von Bohlen und Halbach was chairman of the board of trustees of the "Adolf Hitler Donation by German Business", he became a "war industry leader" four years later and reorganised his company to meet the needs of the war economy. On his 70th birthday, he was honoured with the Golden Party Badge and the War Merit Cross first class for "meritorious service to the armament of the German army".[140] At least 100,000 slave labourers and concentration camp inmates were employed in armaments production at Krupp. After 1945, Gustav Krupp von Bohlen und Halbach was imprisoned as a war criminal. A few days before the Nuremberg Trials began, he suffered a stroke and was deemed unfit for trial. His elder son Alfried, who had assumed management of the company in 1943, being the sole owner, was sentenced in 1948 "in connection with plundering and promotion of slave labour" to twelve years imprisonment and confiscation of his assets. As early as in 1951 he was pardoned and the confiscation of his assets repealed.

Paul Müller

born in Bürrig near Opladen in 1876, died in Würgendorf in Burbach in 1945

Holding a PhD in chemistry, we was general director of Rheinisch-westfälische Sprengstoff AG from 1908. In 1926, he became chairman of the board of Dynamit A.-G. (formerly Alfred Nobel & Co.) that had been founded by Alfred Nobel in 1865. During the Second World War, the companies were two of the largest ammunition producers in Europe and served the German army. Paul Müller was honoured on several occasions in recognition of his services on behalf of the German explosives industry and the German economy. He was a member of numerous supervisory boards and, as of 1933, he sat on the honorary committee of the "House of German Art".

Wilhelm von Opel

born in Rüsselsheim in 1871, died in Wiesbaden in 1948

After the death of his father, Adam Open (1837–1895), Wilhelm von Opel assumed joint management of the family business founded in 1862 along with his four brothers. Adam Opel had begun as a manufacturer of sewing machines and bicycles before his sons brought the group into the automotive industry in 1898. Wilhelm Opel was appointed Privy Councillor and ennobled in 1917. The Opel Works were purchased by the US automotive manufacturer General Motors in 1929. In a report by the Nazi's Main Security Office dated 9 June 1936, it was stated that "Privy Councillor Wilhelm von Opel has a merely representative role and is chairman of the supervisory board of Opel A.G. only because he bears the name of Opel, he no longer has any commercial influence."[141] Opel was a member of the committee of the "House of German Art" from 1933. Following Hitler's declaration of war on the USA, Goering gave orders for the business to be headed by German managers and to be deployed for armaments production.[142]

Fritz Rechberg

born in Hersfeld in 1868, died there in 1939

Friedrich (Fritz) Ernst Rechberg was born into a Hersfeld manufacturing family who had been in the textile industry for generations. In addition to managing his father's business, Tuchfabriken A. Rechberg GmbH, Fritz Rechberg was jointly responsible for the economic affairs of numerous businesses. For example, he was a member of the supervisory board of Deutsche Kalisyndikat GmbH and Commerzbank-Privatbank AG in Berlin, as well as majority shareholder and chairman of the supervisory board of Benno Schilde AG in Bad Hersfeld. Until his death in 1939, Fritz Rechberg was a member of the honorary committee of the "House of German Art".

Philipp Reemtsma

born in Osterholz-Scharmbeck near Bremen in 1893, died in Hamburg in 1959

Building on the industrial production of brand cigarettes, Philipp Fürchtegott Reemtsma and his brothers expanded the company inherited from their father into an important industrial group in the 1920s. Donations of millions of Reichsmarks made to Herman Goering safeguarded the market dominating position of the tobacco empire for the duration of the Nazi period. Philipp Reemtsma was appointed "war industry leader" in 1943. In 1948, Hamburg Regional Court sentenced him to pay a fine of ten million Deutschmarks in connection with bribes paid to Goering; the sentence was revised in 1949.

Ludwig Roselius

born in Bremen 1874, died in Berlin in 1943

A son of a coffee wholesaler, he had developed a method in 1905 that enabled caffeine to be removed from coffee beans. The patent formed the basis for the company Kaffee-Handels-Aktiengesellschaft (Kaffee HAG) founded in 1906 which, not least on account of modern marketing strategies, became a synonym for decaffeinated coffee, capturing the international market within a few years. Ludwig Roselius acted as a patron of the arts and gave particular support to the Worpswede artists around Heinrich Vogeler and Paula Modersohn-Becker. In 1926, he had Böttcherstrasse, a former craftsmen's alley in Bremen's city centre, redesigned as an architectural work of art in itself involving expressionistic structural shapes and Germanic symbolism. In the 1920s, Roselius already sympathised with National Socialism and enthused about folkish-Nordic ideas and the associated concept of the superiority of the Nordic "master race". Any attempt to win over the Nazi rulers for the architectural ensemble of Böttcherstrasse, which was intended to visualise such a world view, failed, however. Hitler stigmatised Böttcherstrasse as "degenerate art" but it was preserved, presumably thanks to intervention by Albert Speer, and put under protection as a historical monument.[143] Ludwig Roselius, who wrote several historico-cultural works on the cultural renewal of Germany, was a member of the honorary committee of the "House of German Art" from 1933 onwards.

August Rosterg

born in Massen near Dortmund, died in Sweden in 1945

As general director and majority shareholder of Wintershall AG, August Rosterg was an authoritative figure in the area of German potash mining. Since the beginning of the 1930s at the latest, August Rosterg publicly supported Hitler and provided him with large amounts of cash. He signed a petition along with other industrialists submitted to President Hindenburg in 1931 demanding Hitler be made chancellor.[144] Rosterg was a member of "Himmler's Circle of Friends" and wrote articles for the "Völkischer Beobachter". He was a member of the honorary committee of the "House of German Art".

Willy Sachs

born in Schweinfurt in 1896, died in Oberaudorf in 1958

Willy Sachs was the son of the engineer Ernst Sachs (1867–1932), the inventor of the freewheel hub for bicycles and founder of the world famous Fichtel und Sachs precision ball bearing works in Schweinfurt. In 1926, Willy Sachs became a member of the board of his father's company and assumed management of it in 1932. Two years previously he had been appointed royal Swedish consul and made honorary citizen of the City of Schweinfurt. Willy Sachs was a member of the honorary committee of the "House of German Art" from 1933 onwards. The same year he joined the NSDAP and became a member of the SS. When he inaugurated the football stadium in Schweinfurt that he had financed in 1936, Himmler and Goering attended the event as guests of honour. Sachs had been an SS Obersturmbannführer since 1943 and subsidised numerous Nazi organisations with large amounts of money – including the Thuringian State Office for Race Questions, which was, under the leadership of the fanatic national socialist and Munich sports physician Karl Astel, responsible for thousands of forced sterilisations.[145] In 1948, the denazification court in Schweinfurt classified him as a "follower".

Hermann Schmitz

born in Essen in 1881, died in Heidelberg in 1960

Since 1925, financial director of I. G. Farben, Herman Schmitz rose to become the chairman of the board of this major company in 1935. "No officer of I. G. Farben," writes publicist and historian Volker Koop in his biography of the company, published in 2005, "opposed the Nazis' policy of Aryanisation [...] With its domestic plants and especially with its international contacts, I.G. Farben was indispensable for the war economy of the "Third Reich". It deployed forced labour, built a synthetic rubber plant in the vicinity of Auschwitz concentration camp and exploited camp inmates."[146] Degesch, a subsidiary of I. G. Farben, distributed the nerve gas Zyklon B which was deployed in the gas chambers of Auschwitz-Birkenau to commit mass murder. Hermann Schmitz was appointed "war industry leader" in 1935 and was awarded the War Merit Cross first class in 1941. He was a member of the committee of the "House of German Art" from 1933 onwards. In 1948, the Nuremberg Tribunal sentenced him to four years imprisonment "in connection with plundering" from which he was granted early release in 1950. Already by the 1950s he was able to establish himself again as member of the supervisory board of Deutsche Bank in West Berlin and honorary chairman of the supervisory board of Rheinische Stahlwerke.

Alfred and Otto Schmitz

The "Schmitz Donation" was established by Hermann Schmitz in memory of his brothers Alfred and Otto who had died in the First World War and was intended to promote cultural purposes. Hermann Schmitz donated 100,000 Reichsmarks from this foundation to the "House of German Art".

Ludwig Schuon

born in Calw in 1871, died in Munich in 1937

Ludwig Schuon was a member of the board of Badische Anilin und Soda Fabrik (BASF) as of 1914. His cooperation was key to the foundation of I. G. Farben in 1926, which he headed as director until 1927. Ludwig Schuon held numerous honorary posts and titles. He was, among other things, honorary professor at the University of Freiburg im Breisgau, Privy Councillor of Commerce and until his death in 1937, member of the honorary committee of the "House of German Art".

Carl Friedrich von Siemens

born in Berlin in 1872, died in Neu Fahrland near Potsdam in 1941

Carl Friedrich von Siemens was the youngest son of the renowned inventor and company founder Werner von Siemens (1816–1892). After the death of his brothers, he stepped up in 1919 to head the company that from the mid-1920s was one of the world's leading electrical companies. In the Weimar Republic, Carl Friedrich von Siemens was a member of the Reichstag (German parliament) for the Deutsche Demokratische Partei and was committed to corporate social policy. In addition, he took on numerous posts and honorary posts relating to science and the arts. He was a member of the committee of the "House of German Art" from 1933 onwards. Just like other major German companies, Siemens AG benefited from the systematic exploitation of prisoners of war, forced labourers and concentration camp inmates. The company's own plant was built in the vicinity of Ravensbrück women's concentration camp in 1942 with 20 production buildings.[147] At this point, the Siemens Group took third place in the ranking of largest German companies after I. G. Farben and Vereinigte Stahlwerken.

4 "Capital of German Art"

4.1 Laying the foundation on the "Day of German Art"

Munich – the city that Hitler made a glowing declaration of love to in "Mein Kampf" – offered the best possible conditions to be revitalised as an "artistic city" under the flag of National Socialism. The "wonderful combination of natural vitality and its artistic atmosphere, this single line from the Hofbräuhaus to the Odeon, Oktoberfest to the Pinakothek",[148] that had already enthused Hitler when he had relocated from Vienna to Munich as an amateur artist in 1913, increasingly framed the cultural self-perception of the city and formed, when turned into a folkish-reactionary attitude, a suitable breeding ground for its future mission as National Socialist "Capital of German Art." Hitler's promise to make the former "Athens on the Isar" for all time the centre of a German art (as defined by him) was initially expressed in the personal care with which he persistently drove forward the construction of the "House of German Art". At the same time, things had happened here that would discredit the "revived" German cultural nation for a long time to come. In April 1933, representatives of Munich's cultural elite, which included among others Richard Strauss, Hans Pfitzner, the director of the Academy of Fine Arts, German Bestelmeyer, and virtually the entire staff of the academy, signed a shameful document in which "Munich the Richard Wagner City" denounced the author Thomas Mann for having denigrated the memory of the composer so admired by the "Führer".[149] On 10 May, books by Lion Feuchtwanger, Erich Kästner, Heinrich Mann, Kurt Tucholsky and other authors declared "enemies of the Reich" were burnt on the Königsplatz to the applause of 50,000 Munich citizens. This precisely planned and organised campaign, which was also staged in other German university towns, was deemed to be the symbolic prelude to a series of barbaric actions intended to systematically exclude undesired, ostracised artists from future cultural and social life. At the end of September 1933, the foundation of the Reich Chamber of Culture

Procession "The Golden Ages of German Culture", 15 October 1933

constituted the decisive stroke of "enforced conformity" and total control of cultural life. Just under three weeks later on 15 October 1933, Munich was given its honorary title on the occasion of the laying of the foundation stone of "House of German Art", which was to be followed in 1935 by its proclamation as "Capital of the Movement". The ostentatious ceremony was part of a two-day programme that was held under the aegis of the Munich-Upper Bavaria Gauleiter's office and entered the National Socialists canon of rituals as the "Day of German Art". The model for this elaborately staged undertaking were the artists' festivals traditionally held since the 19th century and the large-scale events dedicated to the artistic city mythology such as the inauguration of the Deutsches Museum that had taken place in 1925 in the presence of President Hindenburg with celebrations over several days and a procession one and a half kilometres in length. As had already been the case with regard to the construction of the "House of German Art", all Germans "also those beyond our borders" were called upon to contribute in the form of donations to "ensure that these days not only attract the eyes of the German people but send out an echo that sounds the fame of Munich as the most sublime site for art throughout the entire world" wrote the "Münchner Neueste Nachrichten" on 18

September 1933. After the response to this appeal apparently turned out to be rather modest, the tone became significantly sharper. "There are, it seems," read a statement by deputy Gauleiter Otto Nippold published 10 days later, "people even in Munich who deem it necessary to niggle about the generous organisation of the "Day of German Art" [...] They are those all-too-familiar egoists who, when they ramble on about an allegedly "better use for the money", always mean their own stomach for which they are plainly willing to sacrifice everything."[151] Besides all expenditures would completely flow back into the national economy and "had been providing thousands with work and bread for weeks." Nippold then made it known at a press conference in Berlin on 2 October that the costs of the procession on the upcoming "Day of German Art" would be assumed by the entire population of Munich. Similarly, the street decoration had been financed by Munich's tenants and house owners.[152] Irrespective of this declaration, the number of voluntary donors was probably actually rather limited. The undertaking "Day of German Art" finally left behind a deficit of around 145,000 Reichsmarks, which was ultimately settled by the city, the state and the party.[153]

The laying of the foundation stone for the "House of German Art" was, at the same time, intended to constitute the foundation stone for the renewal of German artistic life and to present National Socialist Germany to the eyes of the whole world as a peace-loving cultural nation. Weeks beforehand, a poster designed by Richard Klein had already been sent to all branches of German businesses abroad for advertising purposes. The former student of Stuck, who had adjusted completely to the National Socialist outlook on art and soon counted as one of the artists appreciated by Adolf Hitler[154], fell back on a very symbolic motive for his design. The head of the goddess "Pallas Athena" was seen as the trademark of Munich art exhibitions since the world-famous Secession poster by Franz von Stuck dating from 1893. The motive, enriched with an eagle, burning torch and a wreathed swastika, was intended to symbolise the "deep relationship between art and the power of the new state"[155] and had such a powerful effect that it was thereafter used as the mark of the "House of German Art" and adorned all exhibition posters, catalogues and souvenirs. An English language commemorative volume on the "House of German Art" ("The Temple of German Art") was published by Bruckmann Verlag on the occasion of the "Day of German Art".[156]

The ceremonies began on 14 October 1933 with a press reception in the rooms of the Künstlerhaus ("House of Artists").[157] In the run-up it was proudly announced that just under 100 representatives of all important international newspapers would attend this event and "the world's interest in German culture" had thus been adequately expressed.[158] The official opening of the festivities followed that evening and was held in the concert hall near the Wittelsbacher Palais in which the "Bavarian Political Police" (later to become the Gestapo) had set up its headquarters under the leadership of Reinhard Heydrich. It involved speeches by Munich's Lord Mayor Karl Fiehler and Gauleiter Adolf Wagner and was framed by musical performances by the National Socialist Reich Symphony Orchestra and the choir of the Munich Bürgersängerzunft guild of singers. The celebrations that were restricted to invited guests were broadcasted by radio throughout Germany, as was the laying of the foundation stone the following day. At 8.00 p.m. theatre and opera performances on Munich's stages followed. For example, the Residenz-Theater offered "The Marriage of Figaro", Theater am Gärtnerplatz played "Vienna Blood". At the same time, the Reich Symphony Orchestra put on a concert for the crowds at the circus building on the Marsfeld. All events were both organised and funded by the Gauleiter's office in order "to also allow the poorest fellow Germans to participate" as was announced in the press.[159] Furthermore, there was the possibility to enjoy concerts with standing space at various places throughout the city. The following Sunday began at eight in the morning with a procession of the artistic and student communities, SS, SA, the Stahlhelm and the state police as well as the Hitler Youth and Munich's schoolchildren that led to Prinzregentenstrasse. Police, SA and SS were deployed to maintain order. At 10.30, peals of bells from every church in Munich announced the beginning of the laying of the foundation stone for the "House of German Art" which was heralded in by the prelude to Richard Wagner's "Meistersinger". Hitler appeared in the morning ceremony completely in the role of patron and sponsor of the arts. In his speech, which he opened with the dramatic words "It is delightful to live in a time that presents its people with great tasks" he appointed Munich the "Capital of German Art". It was "a question of justice to elect this of all cities as the centre point of new artistic creativity and cultural life for all time [...] If Berlin is capital of the Reich, Hamburg and Bremen the capitals of German shipping, Leipzig and Cologne the capitals of German commerce, Essen and Chemnitz the capitals of German industry, then Munich should once again become the capital of German art." With this, Hitler made reference to the artistic tradition of the 19th century that had taken its glittering beginning under the patronage of Ludwig I. In line with this, he ended his speech with a paraphrase of a famous quotation of the Wittelsbacher king: "May this city recall its real mission of being a place of sublimity and beauty that is once again proven to be true that a person must have seen this city in order to know Germany."[160] Manifestation of this statement came in the afternoon in the form of a procession entitled "The Golden Ages of German Culture" through the adorned inner city. At the instructions of the highest authority, Munich's craftsmen and artists had, under the direction of architect and academy profession Georg Buchner, immersed the city in a sea of flags, floral decorations, pine branches and red cloth. Galeriestrasse, for instance, shone in the colours of art, white and red, the monument to Ludwig I on Odeonsplatz was – as appropriate for his importance as creator of Munich as a city of art – crowned by a canopy, his surroundings decorated in Bavarian white-blue. At the Feldherrnhalle, the scene of the failed putsch of 1923 and, since Hitler's "seizure of power", elevated to the National Socialist

Laying of the foundation stone, 15 October 1933, unofficial photograph

place of worship, there was an altar with a golden laurel wreath and burning flame. This procession under the artistic and organisational direction of Josef Wackerle und Konrad Hommel[161] was led by timpanists and people dressed in pseudo-historical mediaeval costumes carrying eagles. The emblems of the "new state", the architecture, painting and sculpture were followed by the individual stations of the procession with reproductions of "The Bamberg Rider, Pallas Athena, Gothic style with fountains of youth, Bavarian Rococo with groups representing hunting, fishing, livestock breeding and defensive ability, German fairy tales, German mythology, poetry and the meistersingers." The procession ended with the "carriage of the future" consisting of "youth with flags and emblems" and the Hitler Youth. "But at the centre of everything," the excited reporting went, "there soars, borne by 18 men dressed in green and gold, surrounded by a rich, multi-coloured entourage, the huge model of the House of German Art shimmering with gold, which is being built according to the draft by Paul Ludwig Troost: the House of German Art forms the hub of the Day of German Art and it is therefore right for it to form the focus and highlight of the procession."[162] However, an incident seen to be a bad omen that happened during the laying of the foundation stone decidedly darkened the festive mood. When Hitler tapped on the foundation, the silver hammer produced especially for this occasion broke in two; there had been plans for it to be used thereafter for the laying of the foundation stones of all major construction projects in the "Third Reich." As might be expected, this scene that did not follow protocol was not recorded by the censored domestic press. The unexpected outcome of the symbolic hammer blow did, however, make the headlines of international newspapers. "A Shock for Hitler – Smashed Silver Hammer – Speech Cancelled", wrote "The Daily Mail" for example on 16 October 1933.

4.2 The procession "2000 Years of German Culture"

On the occasion of the inauguration of the "House of German Art" in July 1937, Munich celebrated the "Day of German Art" for the second time and it was planned to be an annual event from now on. "Now the House of German Art is completed, the Capital of the Movement, the City of German Art is preparing for the ceremonial opening that, in line with its significance, not only exceeds by far the pomp of the celebrations for the laying of the foundation stone but will rise to a flame in testimony of peaceful German civilising intent" was the message communicated through the press at the beginning of June. "An extensive artistic programme will raise the three-day celebrations in the Capital of the Movement to an experience nothing like anything the world has ever seen before or is likely to ever see again."[163] The preparations for the event held from 16 to 18 July were to develop into a grandiose business from which Gauleiter and Minister of the Interior Adolf Wagner would not only see financial gain. So as a to be able to go to work with "real National Socialist spirit", he founded the association "Münchener Großveranstaltungen e. V.", which employed around "300 men and women" alone for the organisation and logistics of the "Day of German Art".[164] In addition, the association was to organise all other "events of importance to the Reich" in the city and the region (that were not handled by the NSDAP itself) and thus rise to become one of the largest employers in the city.[165] The main focus, however, was on the "Day of German Art" and on planning the associated procession that was now held – at Hitler's express wishes[166] – under the motto of "2000 Years of German Culture" and surpassed its predecessor by far in terms of effort and expense, scope and propagandistic explosiveness. Although Josef Wackerle was initially under discussion as the artistic director[167], the sculptor Richard Knecht and the artistic painter Hermann Kaspar (who had also designed the stylised meandering swastikas on the roof of the colonnade of the "House of German Art") were entrusted with organising the procession. The two men were awarded professorships at the Academy of Fine Arts in 1938 and 1939, respectively, and were awarded further commissions.[168] Georg Buchner was made responsible once again for the street decorations; Adolf Hitler had already been "very enthusiastic" about the ornamentation in 1933 and had expressed his personal thanks to the artist for his work.[169] It was Georg Buchner of all people who was, after the war, commissioned by the town of Dachau to develop the preliminary design ordered by the US military government for the monument to the dead of the concentration camp.[170]

Already in the run-up to the "Day of German Art", the local press published rapturous reports on the progress of the work on the decorations and arrangements, the products of which were kept in halls erected specifically for the purpose; the costume store in Landsbergerstrasse alone contained some 5000 objects. In terms of Nazi economic propaganda, the event was declared as one of the most important job creation measures and a decisive factor in the economic recovery of

Spectators on the "Day of German Art", 18 July 1937

the Reich. Not only a large number of painters and sculptors from the radius of the Munich Academy were involved in the preparations – no festival, as was observed by the "Münchener Beobachter", had ever before required so many workers and helpers, to the point where "there were no skilled workers available any longer on the labour market."[171] In addition, there were hopes that the "Day of German Art" would also bring about a boom in tourism. Under the slogan of "Everyone to Munich on the Day of German Art", KdF ("Kraft durch Freude") offices offered special trips to the "artistic city of Munich" as well as excursions to the Upper Bavarian sights and places of Nazi pilgrimage.[172] No one in the city at that time would have failed to see how the National Socialists put spectacular amounts of effort and visual propaganda into making these festivities into a celebration of themselves. An informer for the Social Democratic Party in exile reported to the committee in Prague reported: "In May and June already hundreds of craftsmen were employed with manufacturing the figures and sculptures destined for the procession 'Two Thousand Years of German Culture'. In some artistic embroidery workshops, the women worked 12 to 14 hours a day on the wonderful pelmets and fine tapestries. [...] One week before the festival, the flag poles were erected in Ludwigstrasse before the eyes of the astonished people of Munich. The flags, 12 metres long on the 22 metre high poles, were clamped in golden-brown steel tubing frames and hung to the poles on a gallows-like device. Every street along which the procession passed had wire ropes strung over them to each of which three flags were attached [...]

The decorations on the square in front of the station were particularly opulent with more than 200 flag poles being erected here alone. The interior of the station building was lined with red and brown cloths and hung with golden laurel wreaths [...] for the festive illumination on the Saturday, every household had to buy 10 glass candle holders for each of their windows. Anyone who refused had to submit a written justification and file an application for exemption. The result of this was that there was hardly anyone who attempted to get around this order. The illumination was ordered to take place on Saturday at 9 o'clock in the evening. All monuments in the city centre were lit up with searchlights. The technical division of the 'Car Train Germany' alone installed 500 round spotlights. Free concerts were held at ten major squares which all party ranks were ordered to attend. At 7 p.m., the ostentatious reception of the Reich government took place at the exhibition park. The entrance and the whole area were blocked off by the SS. The people of Munich were only able to admire the magnificent fleet of vehicles that could be seen along the access ramp. The streets were vibrant with life. KdF troops pervaded the city until the early hours."[173] In addition to the inauguration of the "House of German Art", the procession "2000 Years of German Culture" formed the propagandistic climax the following Sunday. "Along with the figures from the far and near past of German culture, we ourselves walk as an entire nation in the procession of German skills, German history [...] Every fellow German experiences the great will and the brave achievements of his fathers and mothers, the creative powers in his blood and people," read the foreword of an opulently illustrated programme that was sold for ten pfennigs and contained some thirty pages of information on how to interpret the individual groups in the procession.[174] Access to the procession, with the exception of the grandstands and the cordoned-off standing room, was free of charge. And so stretching over a length of 3000 metres, a large number of elaborately dressed groups trekked through the centre of Munich accompanied by marching blocks of the army, SA and SS[175] in order to present to the open-mouthed "fellow Germans" the

Group portraying "The Time of Classicism and Romanticism" within the procession, 10 July 1938

artistic achievements of the "Aryan" master race" from the time of the ancient Germanic tribes to the National Socialist present day. The city, its buildings, squares and streets acted just as much a background as the frenetically applauding masses of spectators. In a total of seven divisions, National Socialist ideology of a "natural, Germanic elite"[176] linked up to form a vague view of history whose repertoire primarily fed on the Nordic-Germanic legends, German chivalry and heroic sagas as well as set pieces from antique mythology and which saw the rise of the "Third Reich" as its apogee. The penultimate division "the Time of Classicism and Romanticism" that significantly closed with the "World of Richard Wagner" was followed by "Modern Times", which made up the largest group in the procession with more than 1000 participants and more than one third of all contributors. Black knights with the sign of victory of the "national uprising" led this section; they were followed by maidens with burning torches accompanying the sculptural groups

"The Ship of Prehistory" from the group "The Germanic Times" within the procession, 10 July 1938

"faith and loyalty" – two pairs of youths running ahead, naked, who were supposed to glorify the National Socialists' new "pure bred" ideal person. "Mother Earth" and "Father Rhine" were carried along as were models of the "Führer's monumental buildings" which, according to the programme, "were witnesses of the tough struggle for new forms and new mastery of space and area". "At the end of the 2000 Years of German Culture", wrote the "Völkischer Beobachter" one day after the event, "there marched soldiers once again, grey soldiers, brown soldiers, black soldiers. The crowd that had applauded the past centuries had even more applause for the warriors of their own time."[177] From 1938 onwards, there were decided supplements to the groups of people representing the "New Era" that related to current foreign policy successes. For instance, the "annexation" of Austria to the German Reich was celebrated in 1938 with stage imagery which was followed in 1939 by "The Sudetenland", "The Memel Territory" and "The Protectorate", which referred to Bohemia and Moravia. The contributors were mainly recruited from individual party organisations such as the National Socialist Nazi Women's League or the Hitler Youth, or from sports associations, the theatre and cinema. Munich's primary schools delegated pupils to represent "choir boys, dwarfs and torch bearers."[178] On account of the great demand in 1939, newspaper announcements were used to search for female contributors.[179] Special attention was paid to female protagonists in particular. Not only a minimum height of 1.65 metres "but also the figure and the entire outer appearance" were the decisive factors.[180] A former participant remembers, for example, that she was chosen "because of her height and her fair-haired "Aryan" type.[181]

Without doubt the magnificently outfitted processions, the roaring dance and music events the "Day of German Art" provided in its supporting programme were considered by contributors and spectators alike to be a glamorous, apparently non-political, event that they could indulge in elatedly and with naive pleasure, but nevertheless, it did at the same time swear in the masses to the Nazi state and its "national community". The British journalist Isabel Hilton hit the mark with her comment that "the success of the Day [of German Art] was testimony to the power of Nazi mythology. This was gift-wrapped National Socialism, its victims out of sight, its appeal apparently uncontaminated by the existence of a concentration camp in the picturesque town of Dachau, only a 20-minute train ride from Munich."[182] It was mid-July 1939 just under six weeks prior to the outbreak of the Second World War that the "Day of German Art" took place for the last time. "Today we leave aside something that must be kept until a future time of peace: the splendour of the festive days on which people and art may come together in wonderful togetherness – also towards the outside world," read an article in "Münchner Neueste Nachrichten" the following year.[183] Gauleiter Adolf Wagner dissolved "Münchner Groß-Veranstaltungen e. V." in September 1940 as the association was experiencing liquidity problems.[184] Plans and preparations for future events were constantly driven forward, nevertheless. According to a personal request by Hitler "the procession of the 'Tg. d. Dt. K.' [Day of German Art] should only be presented in Munich" and "this material should over time be made from ever better and more precious material for posterity."[185] In 1947 some of the costumes were used by the US military government for a carnival party in Bad Tölz. Some items can now be found in the inventory of Munich's museum of city history.

5 The year 1937

5.1 The first "Great German Art Exhibition"

In the foreword to the catalogue of the first "Great German Art Exhibition", Gauleiter and the Minister of the Interior Adolf Wagner had unambiguously expressed the programme of this show. It was "clear that the only all-German art exhibition" could only show "the most perfect, most complete and best that German art can accomplish". "Anything problematic or incomplete" could "never, now or in the future, have any prospects of being accepted by the House of German Art."[186] As was announced on the occasion of the roofing ceremony for the "House of German Art" in 1935, the motto of this presentation of greatest artistic ability was initially to be "a Thousand Years of German Art". "The exhibition", wrote the "Münchner Neueste Nachrichten" on 1 July 1935, "will have a twofold value. It will show our own people the gigantic size of German art and strengthen its justified pride, and it will also bear fruit for the artists now alive who, under this impression, will liberate themselves from all un-German links, which are still existent in certain places."[187] However, Hitler probably quickly discarded this ambitious project that was soon thematically reduced to "100 Years of German Painting and Sculpture".[188] In June 1936, August von Finck announced at the annual meeting of the "House of German Art" that the building would "in accordance with the Führer's will" be opened with an exhibition of works by German painters, sculptors and graphic designers. The show entitled "Great German Art Exhibition" was to be held once a year from then on and to become "the decisive and trendsetting event for the position of German art of the present day.[189] This meant that the central role, ascribed by Hitler to 'his' building, had been determined. In November 1936 already, a number of artists were invited to participate in the "Great German Art Exhibition" and were requested to "make the best of their artistic work so far [...] available." For the time being, those responsible gave a pretence of being liberal and expressly emphasised that they would give no preference to specific artistic directions or exclude any others. However, "a high standard would be placed on the artistic value of the works submitted."[190] The written invitations were followed by public appeals in the Reich Chamber of Fine Arts' bulletin as well as in daily newspapers and the pertinent art magazines. To date, it has not been possible to establish the names of those who were considered worthy of a personal offer. An announcement published at the beginning of 1937 implies that this may be "a little circle of artists whose works should, in a way, form the cornerstone of the exhibition"[191] and were treated as Hitler's favourites in the run-up. In January 1937, at Adolf Hitler's express wish all "ethnic German artists living abroad" were admitted to take part and the registration deadline was extended to 20 February 1937. The organisation of the "Great German Art Exhibition" as an event where art was sold and the exhibits rotated on an annual basis[192] and the announcement that the works submitted would be judged by a "jury of artists" gave the impression of following on from the tradition of the Munich Glass Palace, which until it was destroyed was one of the commercially most important institutions in the art trade. Even the local "Annual Munich Art Exhibition" – that was put on immediately after the Glass Palace fire as a replacement exhibition and was held in the Maximilianeum as of 1937, under the aegis of Gauleiter and the Minister of the Interior Adolf Wagner – could not close this gap, especially as it was generally only open to artists resident in Munich. It is therefore not surprising that there was an extraordinarily great response to the "Great German Art Exhibition". Not least, this was a question of protecting opportunities to sell and exhibit works and opening up new ones. In total, 25,000 works were registered, of which 15,000 were ultimately submitted. These figures corresponded roughly to the membership figures for the Reich Chamber of Fine Art, affiliation to which had been obligatory for practising an artistic profession since November 1933.[193] Even artists such as the painter Gabriele Münter, who had, as a founding member of the legendary "Blauer Reiter" helped shape the avant-garde before the First World War, decided to submit works for the "Great German Art Exhibition". "I would risk 'Icy Road' right away, it has impressed people with no affinity for art in the past [...] I have the courage to try 'Jochberg'. That is German, a German landscape," Gabriele Münter wrote to her life companion Johannes Eichner at the end of May 1937.[194] However, she wrote from Munich on 22 June to inform him that "the sample sent seems to have been 'met negatively'."[195]

The jury and staff of the "House of German Art", June 1937. In the centre: Adolf Ziegler. In the background, the large sculpture "Comradeship" by Joseph Thorak

The members of the twelve-person jury had been announced at the beginning of May. It was comprised of the following, among others: the sculptors Arno Breker, Karl Albiker and Josef Wackerle, the president of the Münchner Secession Conrad Hommel, the painter Hans Gött as representative of the Neue Münchner Secession, Gerdy Troost, the Austrian painter and later director of the Viennese House of Artists Rudolf Hermann Eisenmenger and the "Reich Delegate for Artistic Design" Hans Schweitzer, who published caricatures in the "Völkischer Beobachter" under his pseudonym "Mjölnir" ("Thunder Hammer"). The chair was taken by Adolf Ziegler, one of Hitler's favourites and "old party comrade" who painted fastidious female nudes and who had been appointed president of the Reich Chamber of Fine Arts at the end of 1936. With the exception of Hans Gött, all of these were cultural celebrities in the "Third Reich." Nevertheless, the judgement passed by this select group did not in any way meet the artistic standards of the "Führer" who had the right to make the final decision. Just under six weeks before the exhibition began, Hitler made a furious appearance. The scene recorded by Joseph Goebbels in his diary happened on 5 June 1937. On this day, Hitler had flown from Berlin to Munich with his Propaganda Minister in order to examine selected works for the "Great German Art Exhibition". After a trip to the "Osteria Bavaria", Hitler's local in Schwabing, they went directly to the "House of German Art", which in Goebbel's opinion, had become "dreamlike in its beauty." "We have a look at the jury's selection. The sculpture is not too bad, but some of the paintings are catastrophic. They've hung up works here that really give you nightmares. So this is what happens when you have a jury of artists. They all look to the school, the names and desire and have mostly lost their sense for the real art of painting. The Führer is fuming with rage. Prof. Troost is fighting like a lion, but she cannot assert herself in any way with the Führer. All the other members of this upright jury make a miserable escape."[196] And so the activities of the "jury of artists" has come to an end. Hitler immediately appointed Heinrich Hoffmann, his official photographer, to amend the selection of pictures; in an atmosphere of congenial unity, he shared Hitler's anti-modernist outlook on art and his preference for the sentimental genre painting of the 19th century. He had already acted several times on a large scale as an "art advisor" and had obtained rare items for Hitler's private collection. "Hoffmann", writes art historian Lynn H. Nicholas "soon proved to be highly efficient in handling the thousands of works submitted; he raced through the halls in a motorized wheelchair and in front of each piece of art he bellowed to the assistants swirling around him a simple "accepted!" or "rejected!"[197] By 22 June the "House of German Art" was, according to Joseph Goebbels, "cleared up."[198] The "Reich Picture Reporter" had allegedly had 500 paintings removed and new ones chosen. After a further visit, Goebbels's diary entry for 12 July read: "It is almost finished and is really marvellous. The pictures that have now been selected are also very, very beautiful, even better than the sculptures. There are not many but suitably selected. The Führer is very happy."[199] Hoffmann, who was appointed professor by Hitler in 1938, was also to be responsible for the selection of the works on display for the coming years – accompanied by Gerdy Troost and Karl Kolb, the director of the "House of German Art".[200] Adolf Hitler's opinion still remained decisive, nevertheless.

How was this first "Great German Art Exhibition" presented in the building that had now been raised to a "temple"? Did this show actually mark the beginning of a new era of German "true" art? When looking at the exhibition catalogue, it becomes apparent that virtually all of the works, paintings and sculptures listed there are stylistically indebted to a conservative academism as was taught at the corresponding institutions since the 19th century.[201] Now and then the influence of New Objectivity became apparent as did borrowings from medieval panel painting. In sculpture, a neoclassicism dominated that grew into militant heroics, mindful of Arno Breker and Joseph Thorak. And so the greater part of the 554 artists in total had already been represented at the Glass Palace exhibition and can be seen as belonging to a generation born around 1870/80. Similarly, younger artists such as Arno Breker (born 1900), Werner Peiner (born 1897) or Adolf Wissel (born 1894), who were the outstanding favourites of "Third Reich" art, had their audience even before 1933. Even the themes that were predominantly shown in the "House of German Art" do not,

Discussion of the "Great German Art Exhibition": Adolf Hitler on the terrace of the "House of German Art", July 1937. Second from the right: Heinrich Hoffmann

"Great German Art Exhibition" 1937; in the background, "The Four Elements" by Adolf Ziegler

at first glance, reveal a revolutionary content. With regard to the oil paintings, landscapes were pre-eminent; there followed pictures of animals, still lifes, portraits and scenes from peasant life and mythology. While portraits of Nazi leaders were in the minority, they were, however, placed in strategically important positions. The image of Adolf Hitler was obligatory and attracted "people's attention" when visitors entered the first room, as was dutifully reported by "Münchner Neueste Nachrichten" one day after the exhibition was opened.[202] Special significance was given, in particular after 1939, to depictions of soldiers and war scenes that clearly fulfilled a propaganda purpose. Soldiers, often portrayed as heroic fighters and in aggressive poses, stood for the ideal of German manhood. They embodied heroism, strength, obedience, willingness to fight and make sacrifices and thus legitimised the use of force and the oppression of weaker groups. In addition, trivialisation of war as "an adventure for men" also served to enthuse the youth with combat spirit and a willingness to fight. In contrast, there were numerous nudes, mainly pained in hyper-realistic style, as demonstrated by Adolf Ziegler in 1937 with his triptych "The Four Elements" that was purchased by Hitler as programmatic wall decoration for the "Führer Building". Tall, narrow-faced women that conformed to the "Aryan" type presented themselves in wanton poses and immediately became, when reduced to postcard format and distributed in large quantities, objects of male fantasy that, in times of war, far from home, was to be expressed as mere voyeurism. "Seen in detachment", reads the summary by Winfried Nerdinger of the works of art produced in the "Third Reich", "these are [...] mainly trivial arrangements; if their functional context is revealed, however, [...] there almost always arises a sophisticated mixture of brutal-male heroism, a portrayal of devoted womanhood presented in a voyeuristic manner that often extends to pornography and a transfigured presentation of the homeland, inwardness and 'health'. It is precisely in this coordinated field of reference that the blood and soil and the National Socialist ideology of domination and oppression is realised; detached observation distorts the decisive functional interaction specifically that even an apparently harmless portrayal of a landscape in connection with a Thorak sculpture [...] becomes a bearer of National Socialist ideology."[203]

With the opening of the first "Great German Art Exhibition" on 18 July 1937 it became apparent that the National Socialist "revolution" in the field of fine arts announced in such a vociferous manner merely constituted a recourse to the academic tradition that had by no way been interrupted before 1933. But in order to emphasise the "Old", which was to visually captivate the masses with an "ideal world" and "eternal truth", as a testimony to a new German cultural life, it was necessary to condemn and eliminate an art form that acted as a progressive and critical factor. In 1941 the art writer Fritz Alexander Kauffmann wrote about the "new German art of painting" that "the German painters no longer paint absinthe drinkers or roulette players, consumptive circus girls on horses, marionette-like ballet dancers, masks yawningly empty or heavily made-up prostitutes. They have no association with the fatal uniformity of slums, city wastelands and doss houses [...] they want to be advocates of positively asserted life."[204] And so Hitler left no doubt that he would proceed as ruthlessly as possible also in cultural matters, using violence if necessary.

In his speech held in the Hall of Honour of the "House of German Art" before "leading men from party and state, army, art and science, commerce and industry",[205] he characteristically only made vague comments about the new German art he demanded, the "standard" for which he saw "in the German people, in its character and life", i.e. in the "Aryan race". On the contrary, he settled old scores in a downright fanatical fashion with strongly detested modernism, its representatives and its patrons: "Cubism, Dadaism, Futurism, Impressionism, etc. have nothing in common with our German people. For all these terms are neither old nor are they modern, rather they are simply the contrived stammering of people God has denied the grace of truly artistic talent and instead has granted them the gift of blathering or deceit. On a later occasion, he commented full of scorn: "Either these so-called 'artists' really see things in that way and therefore believe in what they represent, then one would have to investigate whether their eye defects were caused by mechanical intervention or due to heredity reasons. In the first case, this would be highly unfortunate for these unlucky creatures, in the second case, it would be important for the Reich Ministry of the Interior to deal with the question of at least preventing such dreadful visual disorders from being passed on in future. Or they do not believe in the reality of such impressions themselves but they endeavour to molest the nation with this humbug for some other reason, which would mean the course of action would fall within the remit of criminal law [...] The beginning of this exhibition, however, marks the end of German infatuation with art and thus the destruction of the culture of our nation. We will from now on wage a relentless cleansing war against the last elements causing the decay in our culture."[206] It was revealed the very next day that this was not an empty threat in a way that was as striking as it was alarming.

5.2 The vilifying exhibition "Degenerate Art"

The trophies of the "cleansing war", announced by Hitler like a war cry, hung only a few metres away from the "House of German Art" in the gallery building at Munich's Hofgarten. On 19 July 1937, one day after the ceremonial opening of the "Great German Art Exhibition" the vilifying exhibition "Degenerate Art" was opened in the rooms of the Archaeological Institute (today's Theatermuseum and Kunstverein) In a distorting presentation with a wall-sized abusive commentary, this show condemned some 600 works of art as "degenerate" and pilloried their creators. "The Nazis, practised masters in castrating", wrote John Heartfield from exile in Prague, "have castrated the truth, free thought, the development and the lives of many Germans, and now the painters and sculptors have been chosen as the next victims."[207] The definition of "degenerate" extended to just about any artist who was no longer compatible with the ruling ideology of "healthy art true to nature".[208] With this rigorously imposed cultural policy that Adolf Hitler had outlined at the Nuremberg party rally in September 1935,[209] practically the entire spectrum of modern art in Germany had been liquidated and its representatives evicted from cultural and social life. Even professors and museum people who had promoted Modernism were hounded out of their positions on the basis of the "Law for the Restoration of the Professional Civil Service" passed in April 1933. The artists stigmatised as "degenerate" faced

Entrance to the exhibition "Degenerate Art" (19 July to 30 November 1937) at Galeriestrasse 4

being prohibited from painting and exhibiting; it was not uncommon for internal or external emigration to be the only option. Significantly, one day after he heard the radio broadcast of Hitler's opening speech for the "House of German Art" Max Beckmann left Germany and emigrated to Amsterdam. Ernst Barlach called one of his last wood sculptures "The Horrible Year 1937": a female figure frozen in mourning. For Jewish artists such as the sculptor Otto Freundlich, whose sculpture "The New Man" was displayed in the Munich show and was portrayed on the title page of the exhibition guide, it was no longer only a matter of art. He was murdered in the Lublin-Majdanek concentration camp in Poland in 1943.

The exhibition "Degenerate Art" was not the first event at which the National Socialists defamed Modernism in an outrageous manner. Individual groups of the "Militant League for German Culture" had already been putting on "Chambers of Artistic Horrors" since 1933 in order to publicly mobilise a "healthy national attitude" against unwanted artists and their dealers and collectors. The exhibition "Degenerate Art. Reflections of the Decay in Art" marked one of the first peaks with works by Otto Dix, Hans Grundig, Eugen Hoffmann and Christoph Voll, among others; it opened in Dresden in September 1933 and travelled through German towns and cities as a touring exhibition two years later. In Munich, the show could be seen in the White Room of the former police department in Neuhauserstrasse (today's Deutsches Jagd- und Fischereimuseum) from 4 to 31 March 1936; there were more than 500 visitors on the first day alone.[210] "The end of German infatuation with art" was announced 15 months later with the exhibition "Degenerate Art" initiated by Joseph Goebels and held in Munich's Hofgarten, as could be read in the "Völkischer Beobachter" one day after its opening.[211] This show "The Cleansing of the Temple"[212], which to a great extent adopted the design of the pamphlet composed by Wolfgang Willrich, was an event staged as a deliberate antithesis to the "Great German Art Exhibition". In contrast to the first "Great German Art Exhibition", the planning time for the vilifying show "Degenerate Art" was as short as conceivably possible. It was not until 18 June 1937 that Goebbels had ordered the propaganda show to be held in Munich. It is presumably due to this circumstance that works by sculptor Rudolf Belling were present at both exhibitions at the same time. Whereas his abstract sculptures "Triad" and "Head in Brass", confiscated from the Berlin National Gallery, were publicly defamed at the vilifying show in Munich's Hofgarten, his sculptural

"Degenerate Art". Staged Dada wall with works by Kurt Schwitters, Wassily Kandinsky and Paul Klee

representation of boxer Max Schmeling was part of the "Great German Art Exhibition." This contradiction did not, however, remain unnoticed. The very day after the opening of the vilifying show, the culture press conference issued instructions not to mention the artist for the time being: "The Reich Chamber of Fine Arts has received hundreds of inquiries in this context and will clarify the fundamental issue at a later date."[213] Belling's sculptures were ultimately removed from the vilifying show and were handed over to Bernhard A. Böhmer, one of the National Socialists' leading art dealers, on commission.[214] In contrast, the "Boxer" remained in the "House of German Art". Furthermore, Franz Marc's famous "Tower of Blue Horses" was removed from the exhibition "Degenerate Art" after the League of German Officers had protested against "an officer who had honourably served Reich and Fatherland and had fallen in the First World War [...] being associated with the disgrace of this exhibition".[215] The presence of the four other paintings by Marc remained unaffected by this objection, however.

While the exhibition of achievements in the "House of German Art" generated an almost sacred atmosphere through hanging the exhibits in light, monumental rooms, the exhibition in the neighbouring gallery building was quartered in nine semi-dark, congested collections of horrors. The whole arrangement aimed at suggesting to visitors the frightening and offensive nature of undesirable modern art. In order to shock the crowd, the prices given were those paid during the time of hyperinflation. "The paintings were distributed around without rhyme or reason as if hung up by fools or children", remembers Paul Ortwin Rave, curator at the Berlin National Gallery, in his book "Kunstdiktatur im Dritten Reich" ["Art Dictatorship in the Third Reich"] published in 1949, "... as close as possible to each other, desolately placed next to and above and below each other, high and low, just haphazardly, mixed with sculptures standing on pedestals or on the floor, furnished with inciting captions, explanations or dirty jokes. The wording of the posters and wreaths left no doubt that Willrich, blind with rage, had organised the exhibition because the presentation of the works of art and the words added corresponded to his book. Once visitors had walked up a narrow wooden staircase, they were immediately confronted with a huge crucifixion, the monument for the dead by Gies from Lübeck cathedral, surrounded by harrowing works by Nolde; the title of the room 'Bold mockery of the divine experience during the rule of the Zentrum party'. The next room, a long, narrow passage, mainly served anti-Semitism with abuse of the worst kind in words and images. Then in the general exhibition rooms one saw things like: Insults to women, ideal: cretin and whore, German peasants from a Jewish perspective, this is how ill minds saw nature. It all went on this style, through a show displaying several hundred masterpieces by 112 artists that the initiators wanted to hurt, dishonour, ostracise and damage, destroy them in their labour, their reputation, their very existence." The defamation centred primarily on the painters of "Die Brücke": "Nolde was represented with 26 paintings, Schmitt-Rottluff and Kirchner with 25 each, Otto Mueller with 13. There were 9 or 10 pictures by Rohlfs, Beckmann and Kokoschka in display, 7 or 8 each by Corinth, Hofer, Heckel and Feininger, 6 each by Dix, Mohlzahn, Pechstein and Franz Marc [...] and the 'Kneeling Woman' by Lehmbruck was also included. There were a few foreigners [...] who had similarly crept in, Jankel Adler, Marc Chagall, Wassily Kandinsky, El Lissitzky, Jean Metzinger, Piet Mondrian. Under the heading of 'Such masters taught the German youth until today', there were works by Nauen, Purrmann, Werner Heuser, Caspar, Scharff."[215]

All paintings, sculptures and drawings exhibited were confiscated from the inventory of museums just less than two weeks prior to the beginning of the exhibition "in a lightning operation that took only ten days in the course of which it is said that 4000 kilometres were travelled by car".[216] As authorised by Hitler on 30 June 1937, the Reich Minister of Popular Enlightenment and Propaganda had given Hitler's favourite painter Adolf Ziegler instructions in his capacity as president of the Reich Chamber of Fine Arts to "select and secure the works of German decayed art since 1910 in the fields of painting and sculpture currently in the possession of the German Reich, states or municipalities for the purpose of holding an exhibition".[217] Goebbels noted in his diary entry for 1 July: "Given Ziegler authorisation to confiscate decayed art. He is now setting off with his commission. I hope we can get this done before the Day of German Art. That will be a slap in the face."[218] Three days later the eight members of the commission – that was compiled by Ziegler and included the National Socialist art writers Wolfgang Willrich and Walter Hansen and the "Reich Delegate for Artistic Design" Hans Schweitzer – went to work scouring the German museum landscape both systematically and at their own discretion for suitable objects. 64 paintings, four sculptures and 73 watercolours and drawings were confiscated from the Berlin national gallery alone.[219] "The tour began in the upper storey closed at the orders of the Reich Minister Rust on 30 October last year from which the items on loan from private collections had been removed", reported Paul Ortwin Rave, who had to receive the Ziegler Commission. "The paintings by Schmitt-Rottluff, Kirchner, Pechstein and Nolde hanging in the first two rooms were put on the list without any further contemplation or reflection [...] At Heckel there was discussion, especially about the picture 'Sylt' criticised by Schweitzer (lack of aerial perspective), found not to be serious enough by Ziegler [...] At the painting 'Adulteress', Willrich shouted: He could now finally see the original that he had already published as a disgraceful work. – When I asked them to be careful not to knock any holes in the pictures, one of the gentlemen (Schweitzer?) said: They would still be good enough to burn in Munich, to which another (Ziegler?) responded, euphemistically as it were, they were still not collecting enough for that."[220]

View into the third room on the upper floor. At front right: "The Adventurer" by George Grosz from Dresden City Museum (location remains unknown). To the left of that work: "The Couple" by Ernst Ludwig Kirchner from the Hamburg Museum of Art and Trade (location remains unknown)

Three days before the vilifying show was opened by Adolf Ziegler on 19 July, Joseph Goebbels had turned up along with Hitler for a preliminary viewing. Highly pleased with the results, he remarked in his diary on 17 July: "Yesterday [...] looked at exhibition of decayed art [...] that is the greatest thing I have ever seen. Completely fantastic. We will no longer be considerate of anything."[221] But how did the public react to this event that Adolf Ziegler had recommended at the end of his opening speech, broadcasted on the radio, with the theatrical appeal "German people, come and judge for yourselves"?[222] Did the scandalous presentation and advertising measures such as a red leaflet in lurid design that, inserted in the catalogues for the first "Great German Art Exhibition", invited readers to visit the exhibition[223] actually have the intended effect? The observations of an informer for the Social Democratic Party in exile may be quoted here as representative of a number of contemporary and eye witness reports: "The exhibition attracts huge crowds [...] All levels of the party, schools, DAF, KdF have called for people to visit this exhibition and several special excursions to Munich have been organised from outside. When I was in the exhibition, the majority of those present at the same time were from the lower middle class who can surely be assumed not to visit a great deal of art exhibitions. The reactions were correspondingly naive and without any skills in art criticism [...] In front of the painters of the 'Primitive School' one woman commented to her neighbour in Swabian dialect: 'Anyone can slap on paint like that!' – The other Swabian woman only smiled at this because she didn't know what to say [...] some try to assess what they have seen in a naive fashion. In front of a still life, the subject of which can be identified easily: 'Yes, that's one of the better ones.' Or in front of a picture that depicts a boat from a certain perspective a woman says, 'Oh, that's quite nice!' The man: 'That's supposed to be a boat!' then in a conciliatory tone: 'well, it's not too bad.' In front of a seascape, someone from the coast says laughing: 'he should go out to sea for a start to find out what it looks like.' A picture painted in quite modern style with the caption 'Saxophone' is deemed to be a picture puzzle. Anything that is an exact an image of reality as possible is recognised. Where anything goes beyond this, no attempt is made at recognition; anything that is ugly is rejected [...] The people get most worked up about the huge amounts (figures from the time of hyperinflation) previously paid for such pictures [...] Of course, there are other visitors with a greater understanding who walk in silence through the rooms with a serious expression."[224] The "healthy national attitude" that always confronted the artistic avant-garde with scepticism and suspicion, proved to be a predictable accomplice in this situation. On the other hand, there were certainly visitors among the masses who deliberately took the opportunity of perusing modern art for the last time.[225] According to official reports, more than two million visitors in Munich alone had seen the exhibition before it closed its doors on 30 November. From March 1938 onwards, the show was displayed in various towns in Germany and Austria. In the meantime, Adolf Ziegler performed another systematic "cleansing action".[226] The confiscation was subsequently legalised on the basis of the "Law on the Confiscation of the Products of Degenerate Art" passed in 1938. Some 17,000 works of art by more than 1,000 artists were confiscated in this way, taken to Berlin and mostly sold off on the international art market, often at bargain prices, to bring in foreign currency. The party leadership also helped themselves to works from this collection that were from the top class. For example, Hermann Goering had paintings by Cézanne, Munch, Marc and van Gogh sold off to finance the purchase of "Old Masters" and expensive tapestries for his own collection.[227] It was, however, specifically the sales actions – the most spectacular event of these was the auction of 125 world-famous paintings and sculptures[228] held by the Lucerne-based Fischer Gallery in July 1939 – that made it possible for a number of art works to be saved from destruction at the hands of the National Socialists. For example, Sofie and Emanuel Fohn, husband and wife painters living in Rome, succeeded at the end of 1938 in swapping paintings from the 19th century for works by their endangered artist colleagues. Even during the war, the couple promised to return the collection of more than 200 works to Germany one day. In 1964, the works of art were handed over as a generous gift to the Bavarian State Painting Collections in Munich, Sofie Fohn's place of birth.[229] All in all, the trade in "degenerate" art generated foreign reserves of 681,394 Reichsmarks.[230] On 20 March 1939, an inventory declared to be an "unsaleable remainder" was destroyed in the courtyard of the main fire station in Berlin-Kreuzberg. 1004 oil paintings and sculptures as well as 3825 drawings, watercolours and graphic illustrations were burnt as part of a "fire drill".[231]

6 Art and propaganda

6.1 The "German Architecture and Handicraft Exhibition"

Already one day before the "Great German Art Exhibition" was opened, it was announced that the "House of German Art" would in future accommodate two exhibitions each year.[232] The plans were to put an exhibition on display in winter that was fully dedicated to architecture and applied art – as a supplement to the exhibition of the achievements of contemporary painting, sculpture and graphics. This programme was intended not only to forward the "House of German Art" as the trendsetting forum of fine arts in the "Third Reich" but furthermore provide the programmatic stage for the major architectural projects and plans promoted by the National Socialist state. Correspondingly, architecture, which was one of the regime's most important and most effective means of propaganda, formed the focal point of the show opened in January 1938 and was presented in the form of building models, plans and large-size photographs spread over the entire ground floor of the building, while the two galleries on the upper floor were reserved for arts and crafts. The organisation of the "German Architecture and Handicraft Exhibition" also arose from Adolf Hitler's express wish and was organised along the lines of the "Great German Art Exhibition". At the end of November 1937, "all positions in the party, the state, the army and the general public" were called upon to "submit models, photographs and plans and other suitable exhibition material relating to buildings or building projects and [..] to immediately contact the House of German Art"; the motto was to be "German Architects, German Artistic Craftsmen, Show the People What You Can Do." Similarly, all "businesses working in the field of handicraft" were requested to participate in the show "and to provide really top-class work in the field of handicraft."[233] In order to prevent the store rooms from being inundated, participants were instructed to submit to the "House of German Art" photographs of models and larger works for appraisal; for handicraft products, collection and preliminary inspection points were set up in "every district in the Reich" where employees of the "House of German Art" selected appropriate exhibits. In the "district steeped in tradition" of Munich-Upper Bavaria, this task was performed by the Bavarian Arts and Crafts Association.[234]

Virtually all protagonists of National Socialist architecture and their clients were already represented at the first "German Architecture and Handicraft Exhibition" which was ceremonially opened with speeches from Adolf Hitler and Joseph Goebbels on 22 January 1938. The spectrum ranged from the buildings of the "master teacher" of National Socialist architecture, Paul Ludwig Troost (to whom the first room of the exhibition was dedicated), through Albert Speer's plans for the site of the Nuremberg party rallies to barracks, Hitler

"Great German Architecture and Handicraft Exhibition", January 1938. View into the "Nuremberg Hall"

Youth hostels and "order castles" as well as motorways and bridges. The NSDAP organisation "Kraft durch Freude" (KdF) and "Deutsche Arbeitsfront" (DAF) showed models and photographs of KdF steamers and the seaside resort on Rügen drafted by Clemens Klotz. The handicraft department, whose exhibits were on sale, included items of furniture, jewellery, paper and textile work as well as a wide range of decorative articles from various materials such as porcelain, glass, wood, pewter and silver. It can already be seen from the few exhibits pictured in the catalogue that even the field of arts and crafts, which was now intentionally referred to as "handicraft", had been subjected to a kind of "enforced conformity". Rustic handicraft forms dominated, while it was not uncommon to fall back on neo-baroque elements, especially for jewellery and decorative pieces. The various ranges of furniture were characterised in terms of appearance by the representative "steamer style" coined by Paul Ludwig Troost. Of course, original pieces from the Troost Studio and other workshops given preference by the Nazi leadership were also on show. The first "German Architecture and Handicraft Exhibition" saw 260,000 visitors over its three-month duration. Around one third of the exhibits on sale found a new owner and in this way "good, German handicraft" was taken into the private home.[235] The press especially praised the "moral" success of this show and emphasised that the exhibits on display were met with great acclaim also from the numerous foreign guests.[236] The exhibition therefore fully accomplished its propaganda aims to the extent that the masses yielded to uncritical admiration at the mere sight of the countless large-scale photographs, plans and large-scale models, and were thus sworn in to the construction programme raised by Hitler to an ideology. International acclaim additionally strengthened German self-confidence. In addition, "building work in the Third Reich" became a popular topic thanks to numerous photo reports. The second "German Architecture and Handicraft Exhibition" that opened, at Hitler's instructions, "before Christmas"[237] on 10 December 1938 surpassed by far the first show in terms of numbers and recorded just under 295,000 visitors.[238] Here, interest focused on the plans for "reconstructing Berlin" and models of (admittedly never implemented) major projects such as the "Advanced School" at the Chiemsee and the "Grand Opera" in Munich which was planned to be built according to monumental plans by Woldemar Brinkmann, one of Troost's disciples and a designer of furnishings for steamers, sacrificing the existing historic structure in the area of the Hofgarten. "But you will understand", Hitler announced in his opening address, "that we, as we are now really a popular movement, must keep an eye on the people when it comes to our building work, that we must build halls that will accommodate 150,000 or 200,000 people. This means we must build as big as our technical feasibilities today permit and build for an eternity!"[239] Nevertheless, the full extent of this excessive construction policy that Hitler stipulated personally for the "Führer cities" of Berlin, Hamburg, Linz, Munich and Nuremberg was never revealed to the public. His gigantomaniac visions ran too much against the moral concepts of his "fellow Germans". When a ban on all new buildings that were not vital to the war effort came into effect in November 1939,[240] the plans to hold the third Architecture and Handicraft Exhibition from 9 December 1939 to 7 April 1940 had become moot. The show was cancelled at the end of 1939 without any reasons whatsoever being given.[241] The construction work for the new "House of German Architecture" that was intended to be home to the exhibition sometime in the future, was thwarted by the course of the last years of the war and never came to be implemented.[242]

6.2 The role of Adolf Hitler

For the rest of his life, Adolf Hitler considered the "House of German Art" to be his personal work.[243] The "Great German Art Exhibitions" were "his" exhibitions where he intended to lead artists to excellence with a heavy hand. This was where the statesman became the "artist-curator" who, matching his inhuman political actions, radically laid down his own ideals and standards as law. Even the endless monologues that Hitler held to his staff gathered in the bleak setting of the Berlin headquarters addressed his activity as curator of the "House of German Art". He boasted that "on his walks through art exhibitions [...] he always had everything ruthlessly removed that was not artistically faultless. One would have to admit to his face that when visiting the House of German Art one will no longer find a single picture where one has the feeling that it was not the product of serious artistic endeavour and cannot be hung up here with a clear conscience. He even had pictures by painters who had received state awards from the Prussian Academy removed from the House of German Art if they were not good enough."[244] Even when Hitler himself had officially withdrawn from cultural affairs at the beginning of the

"Great German Art Exhibition", 1938. Adolf Hitler selecting works, on the right: Karl Kolb, director of the "House of German Art"

Second World War and had appointed Joseph Goebbels as keynote speaker, he made his way into the "House of German Art" in order to provide inspiration for the choice of the works intended for the "Great German Art Exhibitions". Consequently, the exhibition director received a request in 1940 to subject the sculptures submitted to an even stricter assessment: "no archaic faces; no Maillol legs" were the selection criteria emphatically demanded by Hitler.[245] In addition, only a few days before the exhibition opened, a number of watercolours, lithographs, small sculptures and oil paintings by at least 29 artists were had to be removed "at the Führer's request", as he deemed them to be "modern".[246] The exhibits rejected as unfit also included pictures by Carl Theodor Protzen, otherwise held in great esteem by Hitler, who had found success in completely dedicating himself to documenting the building of the Reich autobahns in painting as well as an oil painting by the Munich-based animal painter Heinrich von Zügel who had enjoyed fame since the Wilhelminian era and from whom Hitler had purchased works already at the first "Great German Art Exhibition". These two examples alone demonstrate how strongly Hitler was guided by arbitrariness and spontaneous dislike in his decisions. His role at the "House of German Art" was not only limited to that of the supreme judge of art, however. He purchased more than 100 exhibits at the "Great German Art Exhibitions each year. The account books, in which all sales were listed from 1938 onwards, record a total of 1324 exhibits with a value of 6.8 million Reichsmarks.[247] Most of the payments were handled by Bayerische Gemeindebank and the Munich-based private bank Merck, Finck & Co. More than once, part of these amounts were also settled using uncrossed postal cheques and tax credits.[248] In addition to a range of sculptures, Hitler primarily purchased oil paintings from virtually all genres exhibited at the "House of German Art". The highest priced exhibits purchased by Hitler were three oil paintings by the Werdenfels painter Raffael Schuster-Woldan, whose sales price stood at 60,000 Reichsmarks apiece; they included "Life", a florid-allegorical depiction of the three ages, reminiscent of Tizian and Lenbach, that had already been shown in the Glass Palace in 1905.[249] The cheapest purchase was the woodcut "King Henry" by Ernst von Dombrowski that was put on offer in 1938 for eight Reichsmarks and was also purchased by the Deutsche Arbeitsfront, the district air command in Dresden, the construction group of the sea air force command in Kiel and a private buyer from Hamburg. The purchases were primarily intended to demonstrate the "Führer's" almost inexhaustible patronage aimed at controlling and managing national art. 144 exhibits were used as decorations in the extension of the New Reich Chancery.[250] The majority of the exhibits purchased disappeared, however, literally "from the market into the cellar". One "deposit ledger for pictures" alone records 725 paintings, 94 graphic works and 8 sculptures that were in storage at the "House of German Art" between 1941 and the beginning of 1944 and, with only a few exceptions, were successively transported to the Munich "Führer Building" and the salt mine at Altaussee, were the booty from the National Socialists' theft of art was also stored. 22 of the paintings listed in the deposit ledger, primarily depictions of landscapes and still lifes were delivered to Hitler's private flat at Munich's Prinzregentenplatz in April 1943.[251] As early as in July 1937, Joseph Goebbels noted in his diary: "Went to the House of German Art with Magda, bought pictures. The Führer has already taken a lot of nice things, but there is also still a lot to be had. Afterwards, the total came to 50,000 Mk. There are wonderful things among them. I'm looking forward to everything coming."[252] It was not infrequent for Heinrich Hoffmann and Hitler himself to ensure that the artists in question received the highest prices for their works offered for sale in the "House of German Art". At the same time, the authorities did not shun taking action against artists who, acting on their own judgement, had apparently set the price of their works too high. "Such pricing is unhealthy and will, by the inevitable negative impact exerted on the commercial success, primarily affect the exhibiting artists themselves" was a statement contained in a "leaflet" enclosed with the regulations of the exhibition in 1939.[253] As a consequence, the office of the exhibition director then announced that it would also "exert its influence in consultation with the delegate of the Führer to achieve a reasonable pricing" and otherwise "reject the works in question – even if they were admitted to the exhibition by the jury – or designate them as not for sale.

Not least through Hitler's influence, the "House of German Art" had become the authoritative institution for contemporary German art. Between 1938 and 1944, around 7000 artists applied; only just under one third were actually admitted.[254] Prominent purchasers not only held the promise of excellent royalties and further possibilities to take part in exhibitions (such as the Biennale in Venice[255]) but also held out prospects of material favours granted by the "Führer" and his followers. Joseph Goebbels' diary entry for 15 January 1937 read as follows: "The Führer will now approve large tax rebates for all prominent artists. This is also necessary."[256] "My artists", Hitler is alleged to have once assured, "should live like princes and not dwell in poverty in garrets in the way they probably have in mind with their romantic image of life as an artist."[257] As is well known, monumental state studios were set up for sculptors Joseph Thorak and Arno Breker who glorified the superiority of the Aryan race with their colossal sculptures and were two of the leading artists in the Nazi state. On the occasion of the "Great German Art Exhibition" in 1939, Hitler rewarded Sepp Hilz, the creator of sturdy village beauties and robust peasant lads, with 100,000 Reichsmarks for the construction of a studio house in the Leitzach Valley in Upper Bavaria.[258] Eduard Thöny, who as a caricaturist for the (now conformist) magazine "Simplicissimus" once went to war with Adolf Hitler using a sharp pencil, nevertheless received a "life honorarium" of 600 Reichmarks per month for his services as National Socialist propagandist.[259]

The path to the title of professor often passed through the "Temple" of German art. In this respect, instructions were given to the Munich Art Academy in November 1938 to prioritise the artists "who are strongly represented at the House of German Art and whose works have been bought by the Führer" with regard to their appointments.[260] Complying with this request seems to have been all too effortless as the staff of the academy had already withdrawn their application to elect the painter Hans Gött as honorary member in July 1937 in an act of anticipatory conformity because, the argument ran, "a series of pictures also including those by Professor Gött have been removed from the exhibition in the House of Art at the instigation of the Führer".[261] And so Adolf Ziegler and Joseph Thorak, who had been raised to the status of professor at Adolf Hitler's personal wishes and without consulting the college, were followed by another six painters and sculptors represented at the "Great German Art Exhibitions", including the peasant painter Konstantin Gerhardinger who was assigned the status of civil servant in 1941.[262] When Hitler was informed by the director of the "House of German Art" that Gerhardinger no longer wanted to exhibit there out of fear of bomb damage, he arranged for his immediate dismissal from the academy and withdrawal of the title of professor. Not even Gerdy Troost's intercession was able to prevent a prohibition of his name "ever again being mentioned in a German newspaper or magazine".[263] The career of Adolf Ziegler, one of the oldest party comrades and leading "Third Reich" culture functionaries came to a similar abrupt end in 1943. His efforts to attempt secret peace negotiations with the Allies led to the loss of all his positions, expulsion from the party and brief incarceration in a concentration camp.[264]

6.3 Running of the exhibition and its significance

Without doubt, the "House of German Art" was one of the central locations of National Socialist propaganda. But how was this institution actually organised during the Nazi period? How was the exhibition run behind this façade of art, power and propaganda?

The "House of German Art" employed 60 members of staff on average; roughly half in the area of the exhibition and as supervisors.[265] For this (male) portion of the staff, duties during the periods between exhibitions also included the assembly and dismantling work for the "Great German Art Exhibitions" and to perform menial tasks during the assessment of the works submitted. In accordance with traditional role behaviour, the female staff members were mainly employed for office and commercial work. It was their duty to meticulously record the pictures and sculptures submitted each year, to document whether they were accepted or rejected and to handle sales. Neatly lettered index cards and books of account as well as several typewriters of the "Continental" brand that have been preserved in the archive of Haus der Kunst are witness to this day of this world of orderliness and bureaucracy. Upon being hired, all employees had to give their word of honour that they were "of Aryan descent" and a member of the Deutsche Arbeitsfront.[266] Nearly one in three employees was a member of the NSDAP.[267] In accordance with the significance of the "House of German Art" for National Socialist cultural policy, all strategically important positions, from the caretaker through to the director, were filled by party members. As early as in 1934, Karl Kolb, who was 40 years of age at this point, had been appointed managing director of the "House of German Art".[268] With a "small circle of employees", he was tasked with dealing with ongoing administrative work that arose in the course of the construction work and fundraising for the exhibition building.[269] Kolb, who had worked in a similar position at the "Bayerischer Luftverein" [Bavarian Air Club] until 1933, presumably proved that he was fully suited to the job. In January 1937, he was promoted to managing director and exhibition manager of the "House of German Art". From then on, his field of activity consisted of attending to the numerous guests of honour from the areas of politics, business and culture and to accompany them through the building and the shows being held there. Karl Kolb also composed the invitations sent out in early spring to participate in the "Great German Art Exhibitions" and staged press conferences and guided tours at the "House of German Art".[270] In addition, the new head of the institution, who did not have any previous training of any kind in the field of art history, was further entrusted with the preparatory work for the "Great German Art Exhibitions". This included, among other things, a preliminary review of the submitted works, from which, under Heinrich Hoffmann's guidance, a choice (acceptable to Hitler) was to be made. Each year, Karl Korb selected some 40 of the works shown in the "Great German Art Exhibition" to have reproduced as postcards and art prints. Their mass distribution brought in millions for Hitler's personal photographer. Karl Kolb soon achieved a certain position of power within artistic circles. He regularly paid visits on behalf of Hitler to the studios of painters and sculptors in order to uncover new talent for the "House of German Art". As an example, his 1941/42 tour extended throughout Germany, annexed Austria, Bohemia, Moravia and the Sudetenland. "Due to time constraints and

"Great German Art Exhibition", 1940, Hall of Honour

for other reasons, the trips can only be made by motor car", was confirmation given to him by Hitler's personal adjutant, Julius Schaub. "For this reason, a request is made to provide Director Kolb with fuel coupons for the amounts required in each case (approx. 500 litres per trip)".[271] In contrast, much less influence was exerted by Ottmar Endres who had been employed as the sole art historian at the "House of German Art" since December 1936. After his studies in Zurich and Munich where he had written his doctor's thesis on the "Architecture of the Asam Brothers" in 1934, the son of the nationalist publicist Fritz Endres had previously been employed at the Bavaria Army Museum.[272] One of his duties there had been to organise a part of the exhibition of documents and books entitled "Defence of Germany – Battle for the Reich" that the Nazi cultural community had held in the summer of 1936 on the occasion of the Reich conference in Munich. "In the historical narrative, the exhibition intends to provide a lively image of the Germans' ability to defend themselves over the centuries, it thus also give an image of German greatness", Ottmar Endres wrote about this propaganda show.[273] Numerous reports obtained by the management of the "House of German Art" on the young art historian confirmed that he had "the skill of adaptation and empathy" and was "not spoilt in his artistic opinions".[274] At the "House of German Art" Ottmar Endres was responsible primarily for the guide service and the design of the exhibition catalogues that were published by the Munich-based publishers Bruckmann Verlang and Knorr & Hirth.[275]

Whereas the first "Great German Art Exhibition" lasted three and a half months, as of 1938 they had a duration of up to 34 weeks. By now it had become regular practice – also with a view to filling the gap caused by the cancellation of the Architecture and Handicraft Exhibition – to replace works that had found a purchaser over the first few months with works that had, until then, remained in the store. In order to manage the switch-over as smoothly as possible, the building was closed at short notice for several days, mostly at the beginning of December.[276] In the meantime, the number of works submitted multiplied (for example, even in 1943 seven times more works were sent in than exhibited[277]) so that it was probably not very difficult to make the selection of paintings, graphics and sculptures worthy of being exhibited. The "Great German Art Exhibitions" attracted several hundred thousand visitors each year. In 1942, just under 850,000 people saw the exhibition – within a duration of 34 weeks.[278] In that year, 1214 of the total of 1805 exhibits on display were sold generating total revenue of almost four million Reichsmarks. These figures imply that the "Great German Art Exhibitions" had gained widespread acceptance among the broad masses of "fellow Germans". And so there were quite a number of private individuals among the buyers who gave preference to smaller format sculptures, graphics and oil paintings.[279] The shows were not only perceived to be a mandatory cultural programme but also offer diversion and entertainment through art that was felt to be easy to understand. Consequently, the various Nazi organisations put on trips to the "Parades of German Art" – as the "Great German Art Exhibitions" were called in the terminology of the "Third Reich" – thus also reaching masses of the general public who would not usually go to museums and exhibitions. In times where daily life was soon to be determined by threats of bombing raids, overt terror exerted by the National Socialists and dispatches about those killed at the fronts, the "Great German Art Exhibitions" even served as a refuge full of illusions to distract from the ever more terrible reality. Their being held on a regular basis was seen to be a "sign of inner security and confidence" and mobilised people's belief in the great, tremendous

"Great German Art Exhibition", 1940, Hall of Sculptures

"ultimate victory".[280] In order to be able to organise the exhibitions in grand style even during the war years, Hitler had, without exception, all staff employed in the "House of German Art" exempted "from service in the army, the Waffen-SS, the auxiliary police, the security and auxiliary service and similar auxiliary services in connection with the war".[281] Furthermore, in 1943 a number of painters, sculptors and Munich-based skilled workers associated with the "House of German Art" were given the sought-after status of "indispensable". As late as on 5 February 1945, when Germany had already been reduced to a pile of ash and rubble and the war had already long been lost, Hitler gave orders for the preparation of a further "Great German Art Exhibition". The senseless policy of holding out to the end imposed by the National Socialist leadership now demanded total submission to the needs of war even by the employees of the "House of German Art". Correspondingly, the "number of employees classified as indispensable" was dramatically reduced and "only the really creative and therefore irreplaceable workers" were kept on. In all technical professions, the men classified as indispensable were to be replaced by women.[282] As is already known, this was not to be. Instead, the eighth "Great German Art Exhibition" was opened on 28 July 1944. The catalogue that had a print run of 100,000 copies despite the shortage of paper, mainly depicts images of heroic warfare, peasant idylls and nude paintings. The titles read "Before the Enemy Attack", "Homecoming" or "The Day is Still Young". Nevertheless, more than 80,000 people had still visited the show by 26 November.[283] Thereafter, only a few counts were still made. The exhibition was kept running, however, until literally the final hour. The last picture was sold on 24 April 1945.[284] Six days later US troops arrived in the National Socialist "Capital of German Art".

In June 1945, Karl Kolb was relieved of his office at the instructions of the US military government, three months later Ottmar Endres was suspended. Both were classified as "followers" by the denazification court.[285] In October 1945, the US military government commissioned former employees of the "House of German Art" with winding up the remaining paintings and sculptures left in the building that mainly stemmed from the last "Great German Art Exhibition". Among the numerous letters in which the return of the pertinent works was requested, there were also inquiries from artists such as Arno Breker, who succeeded in continuing his career after 1945.[286] From August 1946 and May 1947 onwards, the works were deposited in the store including the purchases by various Nazi ministries that had not been delivered. These were transferred to the "Central Collecting Point" in the former "administrative building" in Arcisstrasse, the largest of this kind in southern Germany for art looted by the Nazis. From here it was relocated several times.[287] The works were returned to the artists or the purchaser only if they presented a political clearance certificate (denazification court ruling). "As you were classified as belonging to the group of followers, there should be no doubt that your sculptures will soon be released", Arno Breker was informed on 6 November 1948.[288] The "House of German Art Processing Centre" was dissolved in October 1949. In 1963, the US Government handed over to Munich Higher Financial Directorate some of the paintings and sculptures purchased by Hitler that were stored in Munich Main Customs Office until 1998. In the meantime, they are part of the inventory of the German Historical Museum in Berlin[289] – as a collection of contemporary documents.

Aerial photograph of the Haus der Kunst/Hofgarten area, taken by the US Air Force on 8 June 1945

7 After 1945

When US troops entered Munich on 30 April 1945 they found a city that had been destroyed to a great extent. “At the end of hostilities”, remembers the second post-war mayor, Thomas Wimmer, “Munich resembled more a living pile of debris than a community in which people live.”[290] The war the country had brought on itself had left behind a landscape of ruins and rubble. The erstwhile symbols of the city, the Frauenkirche church, the Old Town Hall, the Residence and the Pinakotheks had mainly been reduced to debris and fragments of walls. The Deutsches Museum, the Glyptothek and the Lenbachhaus were heavily damaged. While the upper middle class residential buildings at the southern end of Prinzregentenstrasse had been turned into dismal ruins in the hail of bombs of the Second World War, the “House of German Art” had been almost completely spared thanks to its proximity to the Englischer Garten. Something that may seem to be an irony of history was the result of a meticulously elaborate programme of camouflage as air-raid protection. From September 1942 onwards, the monumental façade was concealed behind dark-green camouflage mats; in addition, part of the area of the roof was covered over with artificial treetops that made the building seem like a continuation of the extensive park to mislead allied bombers.[291] Only shortly after the US Army reached Munich, the US military government requisitioned the building under occupation law that was in effect at that time.[292] A US sergeant with a dry “sense of humour” and making the gesture of a victor scribbled his signature in the “Golden Book” of the “House of German Art” on 5 May 1945, in which previously Adolf Hitler, Benito Mussolini and the Duke of Windsor had immortalised themselves.[293] The attitude of the Americans to the architectural testimony of the Nazi regime was, however, primarily characterized by pragmatic considerations. As the temple of art had functioning gastronomic facilities and sufficient space, they set up a club here for higher-ranking officers with a restaurant, dance hall and several shops. “You had to walk through the antechamber decorated with pillars”, reported journalist

Jella Lepman, "to get to the actual dining room, it was pompously decorated depending on the time of year and the festive season. With glaring paper garlands and hollowed out pumpkin lanterns, rows of tinsel angels hovering against the ceiling, huge candles in papier maché holders or a Walt Disney jungle for the children. American kitsch vied successfully with the Führer's kitsch."[294] The Hall of Honour, once the backdrop to Hitler's slavering tirades against Modernism, now hosted "floor shows" with jazz bands and variety performances. A basketball court was marked out in oil paint on the stone floor of the exhibition rooms, a tennis court was set up behind the building. The columned building was exceedingly popular with the US occupying power and was also frequently used for official functions. In 1950, the German-American magazine "The Munich American" even called the structure "the most beautiful building in Munich".[295] In addition, the gastronomical business of the officers' club offered the people of Munich highly sought-after jobs in times of food shortages; these jobs ensured regular meals and thus basic supplies.[296] Soon after the American GIs, Peter A. Ade arrived at the "House of German Art". His

Northern facade of the "House of German Art" with camouflage nets still in place, 12 May 1945

Entrance to the Officers' Club, 1945/46

original plan was to tempt the officer in charge with his father-in-law's sparkling wine agency. But the congenial young man, who had spent some years before the war working and studying in England and France, was immediately appointed interpreter, personnel officer and soon after, the trustee for the building. His duties included arranging the glamorous "floor shows" and to bring suitable talents from the world of entertainment to the "House of German Art". He succeeded in persuading Frieda Sembach-Krone, the directrix of the famous circus to demonstrate her high-class riding skills in the "Hall of Honour".[297] As its director, Peter A. Ade was later to shape the destiny of the building over almost three decades allowing it to become an institution with an international reputation and immense foresight.

In July 1946, representatives of the US military government declared that the building that had been meanwhile renamed "Haus der Kunst" ("House of Art") was to be used only as a museum in future.[298] In contrast, the proposal to make Haus der Kunst the "central office for tourism, as accommodation for all travel agencies and to set up showcases for the world of business with colonnades", that was submitted by the CSU grouping within the city council in 1948, did not meet with any support.[299] The instructions of the US military government initially only related to the west wing; some of these rooms had already been made available to the Bavarian State Painting Collections at the end of 1945. Works from the Pinakotheks that had been destroyed in the war had been on display there since January 1946. "Years will pass before Munich will have a 'Pinakothek' again", wrote Eberhard Hanfstaengl in the foreword to the catalogue for the exhibition "Bavarian Paintings of the 15th and 16th Centuries". "For this reason, our pictures must seek accommodation in a place where many disagreeable things have happened in artistic life, but also a place, we hope, that will receive the dedication that it has lacked up until now from this first exhibition of great masterpieces not only in artistic respect but also with regard to human interaction in general."[300] The exhibition "The Blue Rider" [Der Blaue Reiter] was opened here in September 1949. It was arranged by art historian Ludwig Grote and involved just under 300 works by artists ostracised in the "Third Reich". This memorial exhibition, which attracted great international attention, "denazified" the former "House of German Art", as permanent secretary Dieter Sattler observed in his opening speech.[301] Similar comments were also made by journalist Jella Lepman who had returned from emigration immediately after the end of the war in order to carry out cultural reconstruction work on behalf of the US military government. The "House of German Art", which had remained undamaged, was in her eyes the ideal place, not despite its past but specifically because of it, to put on display a show of more than 4,000 books for children and young people from 14 countries which she had initiated. This was the first ever international event in post-war Germany. "I began critically inspecting the exhibition rooms", she wrote in her memoirs looking back from the perspective of 1964 "and walked through the halls as if they already belonged to us. In my mind's eye, I swept away the boxes and crates, the international children's books would move into this pagan temple and their good spirits would chase away the evil ones."[302] Liberating oneself from the bleak past with confidence, a cosmopolitan outlook and new, democratic

View into the restaurant, around 1947

guiding principles – this was the attitude that was to determine how the building was treated thereafter.

The Bavarian economy also had to reorganise itself under the aegis of the US occupying power. The "House of Art" also proved to be a venue that was equally symbolic and practicable. The revitalisation of German exports were, most of all, intended to bring in foreign reserves for purchasing raw materials and to gain international acceptance for foreign trade. A leading role in the development of export capacities was played by the Bavarian Arts and Crafts Association, which had maintained a permanent sales exhibition highly frequented by the Americans since March 1946. As early as in May 1946, the first export exhibition "Bavarian Arts and Crafts" was opened in a part of the east wing freed up by the US Army.[303] The much more extensive "Export Show. Exhibition of the Achievements of the Bavarian Economy" followed at the beginning of August. This was deemed to be the "first ray of light for Bavarian industry and commerce" to which representatives of the largest US import companies were invited.[304] Handicraft products and traditional costumes were sales hits but these were only on sale to foreign visitors. The crowds were so big, however, that the exhibition was extended to the end of 1948 and was even expanded into further rooms. It was not until the shop windows started to fill up again with goods on sale due to the currency reform, that interest waned.

In November 1948, Haus der Kunst was released from the assets managed by the Allied Control Council and handed over to the Bavarian state. The restaurant, the former "Hall of Honour" and part of the adjoining exhibition and administrative rooms, however, remained under US occupation as an "officers' club" until 1955. In his memoirs, Peter A. Ade later portrayed how he had to show each new mess officer who reported for service in Haus der Kunst the plans of the building "so that they could see which rooms were used by the Americans". He "pinched a room every time" in order to slowly free up the building.[305] This meant that lively exhibition activities were soon able to develop also in the east wing. In the meantime, the local artists' associations, that had been dissolved by the National Socialists in 1938 and incorporated into the "Kameradschaft der Künstler", had reformed and joined together in the "Ausstellungsleitung e. V." The object and purpose of the "Ausstellungsleitung" was to organise the "Great Munich Art Exhibition" and to perform retrospective exhibitions of classical modernism and cultural history shows (such as the "International Film Exhibition" in 1958 or "Tutankhamun" in 1980).

Fashion show at the "Export Show", August 1946

In September 1949 had already, the "Neue Gruppe", "Secession" and the "Münchener Künstler-Genossenschaft" held their first "Great Art Exhibition" in which Max Beckmann, Karl Schmitt-Rottluff and Otto Dix, among others, also participated. This form of autonomous presentation of art, that follows the tradition of the Glass Palace presentations and offers up-and-coming and well-known artists alike a crucial forum for their work, continues to this day. The same year, this association began its carnival parties – by now legendary – that made Haus der Kunst a carnival stronghold for 25 years not only thanks to the swing performed by band leaders such as Max Greger, Hugo Strasser and Ernst Jäger. With huge installations and paintings that, with their expressive air, were reminiscent of the Modernism ostracised as "degenerate", Munich's art scene turned the marble halls into wild landscapes, palaces and alehouses, thus occupying the building burdened by history in their own way.

Since the 1950s, Haus der Kunst has developed into one of the most renowned places in the international art industry. The large-scale

View into the Emil Nolde exhibition, 1957

Visitors in front of Picasso's "Guernica", 1955

solo exhibitions were mainly dedicated to artists such as Frank Lloyd Wright, Ernst Ludwig Kirchner, Emil Nolde, Le Corbusier, Oskar Kokoschka, Vincent van Gogh or Wassily Kandinsky and Paul Klee. Many of these shows "thus made a form of moral amends in the cultural context."[306] In this way, artistic works, that had been stigmatised by the National Socialists as "degenerate" and had been removed from the collections, were made accessible for the first time to visitors. It was here that Picasso's antifascist tableau "Guernica" was on view in 1955 – the first time in Germany – which had been created in 1937 under the impression of the destruction of the Basque city of the same name by German aerial bombardment – "unprotected, unguarded, without armoured glass", as Peter Raue remembers 50 years later.[307]

In 1962, 25 years after the opening of the vilifying show "Degenerate Art" in Munich's Hofgarten, an exhibition held at Haus der Kunst was the first time visitors were reminded of the unprecedented iconoclasm of the National Socialists. Just as symbolic as the venue was the fact that the artists Otto Dix, Oskar Kokoschka, Hans Purrmann and Karl Schmitt-Rottluff were won over as members of the honorary committee; their works had been publicly defamed in 1937. "Degenerate Art – Iconoclasm 25 Years Ago" displayed around 350 works that

Joseph Beuys while the installation "The End of the 20th Century" is being erected, February 1984

had been confiscated from German museums during the Nazi regime and condemned as "degenerate" and was intended to be "an admonition, an impressive mark of emphatic and contemplative commemoration".[308] The exhibition was not a reconstruction of the vilifying show of 1937, however. Such a reconstruction came 25 years later on the occasion of the 50th day of remembrance; it was performed by art historian Mario Andreas von Lüttichau and was the basis of the exhibition "Degenerate Art: Documentation of the National Socialist Iconoclasm carried out on the Inventory of the State Gallery of Modern Art in Munich", that was put on display in the west wing of Haus der Kunst in 1987. The State Gallery of Modern Art had moved in there in 1980 – and thus the works of those artists over whose downfall Hitler had in his time hoped to triumph.[309] It was here that Joseph Beuys constructed his monumental work "The End of the 20th Century" from 44 blocks of solid basalt in 1984, two years before his death.

8 Stiftung Haus der Kunst

At the end of the 1980s there were public discussions about a topic that had long been a taboo. It was triggered by the poor structural state of Haus der Kunst which caused the press to post the question "Should the buildings from the Nazi period simply be torn down?"[310] and led to headlines such as "After dilapidation, the great explosion?"[311] The Munich architect Stephan Braunfels contributed the proposal of blowing up the neoclassical building and replacing it with a new two-storey building instead. Others like the author and art collector Lothar Günther Buchheim argued to the contrary that Haus der Kunst was an "important monument"[312]. What followed was not a "great explosion" but partial restoration and, in 1992, the creation of the Stiftung Haus der Kunst gGmbH foundation based on a model of public and private financing. The public controversy about the future of the building not least reflected discussions about how to deal with the architectural remains of the Nazi period. As early as the mid-1960s the state architectural committee had briefly spoken out in favour of complete demolition of the building. The urban development argument behind this was the extension of the Altstadtring Nord road link.[313]

Christoph Vitali, director of the foundation from 1993 to 2003, continued along the path taken by the "Ausstellungsleitung". His first exhibition "Elan Vital or the Eye of Eros" was a perfect example of a programme that put the limelight on the art of classical modernism and at the same time took account of select positions in contemporary art. He staged thematic shows such as "The Night" as sensual experiences. In the 1993/94 the exhibition "Resistance – Concepts for the Future", curated in cooperation with the State Gallery of Modern Art, drew on contemporary artists such as Ida Applebroog, Christian Boltanski, Bruce Naumann or Rosemarie Trockel to also give their views on the building's Nazi past.[314] Christian Boltanski, for example, covered the southern façade of the building with posters of enlarged pairs of eyes of members of the antifascist resistance group "Rote Kapelle" that was largely unknown in Germany at that time. From awareness of the significance of the exhibition building in the Nazi period, he used his installation "Résistance" to confront visitors with remembrance of people who fought against the unjust National Socialist regime thus constantly exposing themselves to mortal danger. The neoclassical façade of Haus der Kunst suddenly appeared to consist of hundreds of pairs of eyes that looked down on passers-by walking along – as a warning and call for reflection.

In the new millennium, there is even greater emphasis on commitment to contemporary positions. The former "Hall of Honour", at one time designated by the Nazi rulers to be used as an empty backdrop of power, is becoming an experimental field and laboratory for national and international projects. Structural changes in the interior that were seen as "architectural denazification" of the building after the war and were intended to cover up memories of the unpleasant inheritance, were undone again as part of the "Critical Reconstruction" project initiated by Christoph Vitali's successor Chris Dercon in order to bring the origins of the erstwhile National Socialist temple of art to light. [315]

The challenge of the location stems from its history that is being countered in a proactive way and at various levels. The US artist Paul McCarthy put the most extensive show of his works in Europe to date on display here in summer 2005 – an attack on the values of the "American Way of Life" and a society manipulated by the media. McCarthy made Haus der Kunst into a surreal adventure park, the components of which also made direct reference to the burdens of the history of the location. He installed a colossal bouquet of flowers on the roof. The sturdy rubber blossoms proved to be far stronger and tougher in their aesthetic impact than the rigid arrangement of columns and made the monumental building shrink to a mere flowerpot from which German balcony geraniums were growing. Two years previously the Canadian collector and curator Ydessa Hendeles had put on, for the first time outside of Toronto, excerpts from her unique collection of contemporary concept art, photographic documentation, anonymous amateur photographs and everyday items. In three passages, "Partners" told a subjective story of the 20th century on random and fateful links. For Hendeles, born in 1948 as the daughter of survivors of the Shoah in Germany, the invitation to curate an exhibition for Haus der Kunst meant a renewed encounter with the land of her parents' traumas: "It also puts me in the position to give my voice a place in my country of origin. The exhibition I put together

Installation "Résistance" by Christian Boltanski on the facade of the building, 1993/94

Maurizio Cattelan, "Him". View into the exhibition "Partners", 2003

invites the viewer to contemplate the change in significance of images in our cultural history on the basis of a series of narrative passages, scenes of wishing and disappointment, murder and suicide, power and powerlessness as well as sabotage and survival."[316] One of the exhibits showed a little figure kneeling down piously in the emptiness of the monumental room. On its slender shoulders rested the countenance of Adolf Hitler. Maurizio Cattelan had him return to Haus der Kunst as a pitiful dwarf.

For Gustav Metzger, who grew up in Nuremberg as the fifth child of a Jewish family and escaped to England from Nazi Germany together with his older brother in 1939, the history of the place, interwoven with his own biography, was also decisive in presenting an installation at Haus der Kunst in spring 1999.[317] The work bore the double title "Travertine / Judenpech". Metzger sealed the granite floor in front of the entrance to the Haus der Kunst with a 60 square metre layer of asphalt, a construction material that was in former times called "Judenpech" ("Jews' pitch" – also a pun in German on "bad luck") a term with clear anti-Semitic undertones. "The most profound experience I had in Nuremberg" Gustav Metzger explains in an interview "was that I knew that, as a Jew, I would never go to the theatre. I walked past, could see photos of the performances, but would always remain outside, at the perimeter. I stayed outside here, too, on the threshold of Haus der Kunst. But today I can change things, at that time I could do nothing. I can make a change to this great building. This also constitutes making a change to history."[318]

The assumption of office by Okwui Enwezor as director of Haus der Kunst in October 2011 gave a new stimulus to ideas on how to handle the history of the building. He was responsible for the initiative to develop new formats for the presentation of historical materials and how to convey them. Similarly, critical engagement with the architecture and its historical context continues. With the opening of the western staircase, the Central Hall now relates, for the first time since the 1950s, to the stairs and rooms leading off from it. It is the central forum and the resonance chamber in which a programme opens up to visitors by means of which Haus der Kunst underscores the fact that the lines of development in contemporary art run at a number of global layers and cannot be subject to geographical, conceptual and cultural constraints.

On the occasion of its 75th anniversary in 2012, Haus der Kunst conceived the exhibition "Histories in Conflict: Haus der Kunst and the Ideological Uses of Art, 1937-1955".[319] Two rival perspectives clashed at this exhibition: National Socialist propaganda of pure German art in the annual "Great German Art Exhibitions" between 1937 and 1944 and the defamation of the artistic avant-garde in the exhibition "Degenerate Art" in 1937. While research so far centred on the period of the "Third Reich", Haus der Kunst took the period from 1937 to 1955 into consideration with this exhibition. Over these first 18 years of its history that began with the ideology of the National Socialists and ended with the transformation of West Germany into a democratically organised state, the political and societal situation changed decisively and pointed the way for Haus der Kunst's orientation today as an international exhibition building for contemporary

Exhibition "Histories in Conflict": Haus der Kunst and the Ideological Uses of Art 1937–1955", view of installation, 2012. In the foreground, "The Four Elements" by Adolf Ziegler (1937).

art. Both the contradictory outlooks on art over this period of time were represented in renowned large-scale international exhibitions: In 1937, a model of the "House of German Art" was on display in the German pavilion at the Paris World Exhibition; with documenta 1 in 1955 Arnold Bode succeeded in making the connection to international modernism with artists who had been condemned as "degenerate" in the "Third Reich". The exhibition retraced this development and investigated the historical inheritance of Haus der Kunst in a national and – also for the first time – international context. The works of art on display in "Histories in Conflict" acted, as it were, as contemporary witnesses of the eventful and burdened history of Haus der Kunst. One important criterion for the selection of works was that the paintings, graphics and sculptures had to have been on display in Haus der Kunst between 1937 and 1955 or in the vilifying show "Degenerate Art" displayed in 1937. One of the curators' aims was to use artistic means to supplement the documentation of the institution's own history. In this context, Haus der Kunst invited the Swiss concept artist Christian Philipp Müller to develop a dramatic composition on the history of the building. Müller's narrative obstacle course and interventions were not restricted to the exhibition area of Haus der Kunst's northern gallery alone – on the contrary, he involved the entire building thus making reference to the multi-layered process of dealing with the historical burdens of the building. The colourfully painted nets that hung like camouflage nets from prominent places on the façade were, for example, reminiscent of the fact that the "House of German Art" was so well camouflaged during the final years of the war that it remained unharmed by bomb damage. Its original meaning was reversed in the exhibition, however: Instead of aiming at invisibility, the colourfulness of these nets aimed at increased perception and strengthened the visual presence of the building in the urban space.

With the establishment of a permanent archive gallery in March 2014, Haus der Kunst has now integrated its history, large parts of which were long suppressed, into its exhibition areas on a continual basis. With this new exhibition format that is committed to research into the building's eventful history and mediating it to a wide audience, the generally static connotation of the term archive is intended to be successively directed into an open and dynamic form. This project is based on the inventory of the Historical Archive which was sifted and made accessible in 2004 as part of the "Critical Reconstruction" which intentionally redirected the questions directed at architecture and inheritance.[320] Set up in an exhibition room that is accessible from the Central Hall in the middle, the archive gallery constitutes the visible memory of the eventful history and the complex historical process that gave rise to Haus der Kunst in the form it has today and that has continued to this very day. In this way, awareness of the historical location is expressed in disclosure of its past and offers at the same time the starting point for reflecting on the present.

Annex

Notes

1 [st.], Eine nationale Katastrophe, in: Bayerische Staatszeitung, 7/ 8 June 1931.

2 Since 1889, the Munich Artists Cooperative, officially formed in 1868, had held the Annual Munich Exhibition in the Glass Palace in addition to the international art exhibitions organised every four years. In 1892, the Munich Artists Cooperative and the "Secession", which had split off from the former that year, still put on a joint exhibition. The Secessionists, who had their own domicile from 1898 to 1916 at the Royal Art and Trade Exhibition Building at Königsplatz (built by Adolf Ziebland in 1838/48), returned to the Glass Palace several times between 1901 and 1917. From 1920 onwards, all of Munich's artists' associations and groups were represented at the Glass Palace.

3 cf. catalogue of the Munich Art Exhibition in the Glass Palace 1931, Munich 1931.

4 Eugen Roth, Der Glaspalast in München. Glanz und Ende 1854-1931, Munich 1971, p. 82.

5 [st.], Eine nationale Katastrophe, op. cit.

6 An den Ruinen des Glaspalastes, in: Bayerische Staatszeitung, 9 June 1931.

7 Hans Bürgin / Hans-Otto Mayer, Thomas Mann. Eine Chronik seines Lebens, Frankfurt am Main 1974, p. 108.

8 Meeting of the city council on 9 June 1931, Munich City Archive, minutes of the city council.

9 Munich police department to the State Ministry of Teaching and Cultural Affairs, 16 June 1931. Archives of the Bavarian State, MK 14348.

10 ibid.

11 Expertise by the forensic chemistry investigation unit of the medical committee of Munich University of 7 June 1931. Archives of the Bavarian State, MK 14348.

12 Munich Building Authority to the government of Upper Bavaria, 10 August 1931. Archives of the Bavarian State, MK 14348.

13 Government of Upper Bavaria to State Ministry of Teaching and Cultural Affairs, 19. August 1931. Archives of the Bavarian State, MK 14348.

14 cf. Wend Fischer, Glaspalast, 1854, in: dto. (ed.), Die andere Tradition. Architektur in München von 1800 bis heute, Munich 1981, p. 47 et seq.

15 cf. Klaus Bäumler, Glaspalast, München, in: Historisches Lexikon Bayerns, URL: www.historisches-lexikon-bayerns.de/artikel/artikel44720 [last called up on 1 September 2015]

16 Letter from Minister of State Ludwig von der Pfordten to King Maximilian II, 18 October 1856. Archives of the Bavarian State, OBB 8946.

17 cf. Exhibition catalogue Aufbruch zur modernen Kunst 1869–1958, Munich 1958.

18 Julius Wolfgang Schuelein, Heitere Hoffnungslosigkeit, Horn no date, p. 50 et seq.

19 Wilhelm Hausenstein, Zur königlichen Stiftung, in: Münchner Neueste Nachrichten, 19 February 1918.

20 cf. Winfried Nerdinger, Projekte und Wettbewerb zur Bebauung des Alten Botanischen Gartens, in: Exhibition catalogue to Munich's museum of city history, Die Zwanziger Jahre in München, Munich 1979, p. 467 et seq.

21 Letter from the Bavarian State Ministry for Teaching and Cultural Affairs to the committee of the Munich Artists Cooperative, 17 July 1931. Archives of the Bavarian State, MK 14348.

22 cf. replies from the respondents as assessed in October 1931. Archives of the Bavarian State, MK 41267.

23 Bavaria State Ministry for Teaching and Cultural Affairs to Adolf Abel, 24 November 1931. Archives of the Bavarian State, MK 14348.

24 Winfried Nerdinger, Projekte zum Neubau eines Kunstausstellungsgebäudes im Gelände des Alten Botanischen Gartens, in: exhibition catalogue Münchner Stadtmuseum, Die Zwanziger Jahre in München, op. cit., p. 476 et seq.

25 Winfried Nerdinger, Adolf Abel, in: Allgemeines Künstlerlexikon, ed. Günter Meißner, Leipzig 1983, p. 113.

26 Die Architekten fordern Wettbewerb, in: Münchner Neueste Nachrichten, 30 November 1931.

27 Völkischer Beobachter, 20/21 December 1931.

28 Bayerische Staatszeitung, 31 July 1932.

29 Adolf Abel, Erläuterungsbericht zum Vorentwurf für den neuen Glaspalast in München, München 1932, p. 6.

30 Werner Hegemann, Adolf Abels Vorentwurf für einen neuen Münchener Glaspalast, in: Monatshefte für Baukunst und Städtebau, Vol. 16, Berlin 1932, p. 437.

31 Alexander Heilmeyer, Glaspalast und Konzerthaus, in: Münchner Neueste Nachrichten, 10 May 1932.

32 Quoted in: Georg Steinlein, Der Wettbewerb für den Neubau eines Kunstausstellungsgebäudes in München, in: Die Bauzeitung, 5 February 1933, p. 42. – The jury included architects Theodor Fischer, Robert Vorhoelzer, Fritz Beblo and museum directors Friedrich Dörnhöffer and Eberhard Hanfstaengl.

33 Depicted in Georg Steinlein, Der Wettbewerb für den Neubau eines Kunstausstellungsgebäudes, loc. cit. – Here also further prizes awarded.

34 Agreement between the State Ministry for Teaching and Cultural Affairs and the architect, ord. Professor at the Technical College in Munich Adolf Abel, 20 December 1932. Archives of the Bavarian State, MK 41268.

35 Villa Waldberta, eds. Culture Department of the City of Munich no date, p. 20.

36 Richard Hendschel: Einige Erlebnisse und Erfahrungen im Kunstreferat aus den Jahren 1913–1933. Auszüge aus den Lebenserinnerungen des Ministerialdirektors a. D. Richard Hendschel. Duplicated manuscript, no place of publication, no date, p. 31 et seq. Monacensia Literary Archive and Library Munich.

37 Letter from Hönig to acting Minister of Education and the Arts Hans Schemm, 18 March 1933, Archives of the Bavarian State, MK 41269.

38 Richard Hendschel, Einige Erlebnisse und Erfahrungen im Kunstreferat, op. cit, p. 31 et seq. – soon thereafter, in spring 1933, Richard Hendschel was the first higher-ranking official to be prematurely removed from office and sent into retirement in September.

39 Walther Schwerdtfeger, Paul Ludwig Troost, in: Neues Münchener Tageblatt, 18 August 1938. Munich City Archive, collection of newspaper clippings.

40 Paul Ludwig was born in Elberfeld on 17 August 1878. For his biography, cf. Thieme / Becker, Troost, Paul Ludwig, in: Allgemeines Lexikon der Bildenden Künstler. Von der Antike bis zur Gegenwart. Founded by Ulrich Thieme and Felix Becker. Vol. 33, Leipzig 1939, p. 427 et seq. and Patrick Utermann, Der Ozeandampfer "Europa" 1926–1930 und sein Innenausbau durch Paul Ludwig Troost. Ein Beitrag zum Stil der Zwanziger Jahre, Munich 1988, p. 116–127. Cf. also the documents from Troost's estate in the manuscript department of the Bavarian State Library in Munich.

41 Julius Meier-Graefe, Ein modernes Milieu, in: Die Kunst, 1901 (Vol. 4), p. 249.

42 The Jewish artist Benno Becker lived in the house at Maria-Theresia-Strasse 26 until his death in 1938. The heirs were then forced, under pressure from the NSDAP, into a compulsory sale of the property for a price far under its actual value. The new owner was Hitler's later secretary Martin Bormann, who wanted to convert the building into an NSDAP guest house. The work required was to be performed by Gerdy Troost's studio. In 1950, the house was returned to Benno Becker's daughter, who later sold it. The building was demolished in 1969.

43 Paul Ludwig Troost built a residential building for Felix von Rath at Georgenstrasse 3 in 1905; it is now under protection as a historical monument. The Kupelwieser house built in Munich's Herzogpark in 1912/13 has also remained intact. Hugo Bruckmann engaged Paul Ludwig Troost as an interior architect on several occasions since 1905 and in 1912 for a draft of a block of flats that was never realised.

44 One exception was the "Bremen" that was fitted out by Rudolf Alexander Schröder. Cf. affidavit by the director of Norddeutscher Lloyd relating

to the proceedings of the denazification court pertaining to Mrs. Gerdy Troost, Bremen, 14 May 1947. Archives of the Bavarian State, Munich, Denazification Court Box 1844 – Troost, Gerdy.

45 Franz Arens, Die Innenarchitektur auf den Dampfern der norddeutschen Lloyd, in: Deutsche Bauzeitung 1925, p. 17 – dto: Baukunst 1930, p. 219.

46 Quoted in Utermann, Der Ozeandampfer "Europa", op. cit, p. 119.

47 Paul Ludwig Troost to Hans Barth, Kiel, 7 October 1926. Paul Ludwig Troost's estate (Ana 325, Case 1), Bavarian State Library in Munich, manuscript department.

48 Cf., as an example, the diary entries of painter Hans Gött, who often made music and went to the opera with Troost, in: Werner Zinkand / Nina Raffalt, Hans Gött 1883–1974. Leben und Werk, Munich 2000.

49 A mocha cup designed by Troost in 1904 can be found today in Munich's museum of city history, described in: Die Prinzregentenzeit. Katalog der Ausstellung im Münchner Stadtmuseum, Munich 1988, p. 441. – As of 1908, Troost worked with the manufactory on a fixed basis. Cf. affidavit by Dr. Fritz Bäuml, Munich, 10. October 1947. Archives of the Bavarian State, Munich, Denazification Court Box 1844 – Troost, Gerdy.

50 In 1897, Martin Dülfer was one of the persons responsible for the department of craftwork at the VII International Art Exhibition in the Glass Palace from which the "Committee for Art and Handicraft" was constituted which, in turn, formed "Vereinigte Werkstätten für Kunst und Handwerk" in 1898. From 1910 onwards, Paul Ludwig Troost worked with Vereinigte Werkstätten on a fixed basis and also designed representative ranges of furniture for them.

51 Patrick Utermann: Der Ozeandampfer "Europa", op. cit., p. 121. – Utermann bases this claim on a statement by Gerdy Troost. Other sources refer to a chest of drawers that Hitler allegedly bought "long before 1933" – Angela Schönberger, Die neue Reichskanzlei von Albert Speer. Zum Zusammenhang von nationalsozialistischer Ideologie und Architektur, Berlin 1981, p. 126.

52 Cf. entry in property tax transfer book / Briennerstr. 45. Archives of the Bavarian State, Munich, land register 12680.

53 München – "Hauptstadt der Bewegung". Catalogue of exhibition of the same name in Munich's museum of city history, Munich 2002, p. 175 – here also an illustration of a draft drawing by Troost. For the "Brown House" cf. Ulrike Grambitter, Vom "Parteiheim" in der Brienner Strasse zu den Monumentalbauten am "Königlichen Platz". Das Parteizentrum der NSDAP am Königsplatz in München, in: Bürokratie und Kult. Das Parteizentrum der NSDAP am Königsplatz in München, ed. Iris Lauterbach, Munich 1995, s. 61 et seq.

54 The monument was removed by the US Army in May 1945 and molten down for the reconstruction of the residence.

55 Albert Speer, Erinnerungen, Munich 2005, p. 53 et seq.

56 Notes made during the interrogation of Gerdy Troost on 21 January 1947.

Archives of the Bavarian State, Munich, Denazification Court Box 1844 – Troost, Gerdy.

57 Paul Ludwig Troost to Walther Troost, 21 January 1932. Estate of Paul Ludwig Troost (Ana 325, Case 1), Bavarian State Library, manuscript department.

58 Draft letter by Gerdy Troost of 11 December 1934. Estate of Paul Ludwig Troost (Ana 325, Case 4), Bavarian State Library Munich, manuscript department.

59 Vgl. Ulrike Grambitter, Vom "Parteiheim" in der Brienner Strasse zu den Monumentalbauten am Königlichen Platz, op. cit., p. 63 (note 20).

60 Im Kampf der Kunst um die Seele des deutschen Volkes, in: Münchner Neueste Nachrichten, 11 June 1933.

61 Cf. meeting of the city council of 24 August 1933. Munich City Archive, minutes of the city council.

62 G. Steinlein, Paul Ludwig Troost, ein deutscher Baumeister, in: Deutsche Bauzeitung, 15 May 1933, p. 171.

63 Archives of the Bavarian State, MK 43329. Likewise, Karl Arndt, Die Münchener Architekturszene 1933 / 34 als ästhetisch-politisches Konfliktfeld, in: Bayern in der NS-Zeit III, Munich 1981, p. 485 et seq.

64 Alexander Heilmeyer, in: Münchner Neueste Nachrichten, 22 January 1934.

65 The first award winner still alive was Alfred Rosenberg. The second prize was awarded to the two surgeons August Bier and Ferdinand Sauerbruch. Third price went to Wilhelm Fischner's explorers. The German National Prize was endowed as a counteraction to the awarding of the Nobel Peace Prize to Carl von Ossietzky. According to this, "it was therefore forbidden for all time for Germans to accept the Nobel Prize". Cf. Die Verleihung des Deutschen Nationalpreises, in: Münchener Zeitung, 8 September 1937. Munich City Archive, collection of newspaper clippings.

66 Meeting of the city council of 18 October 1934. Munich City Archive, minutes of the city council.

67 Meeting of the city council of 20 November 1934. Munich City Archive, minutes of the city council.

68 Albert Speer, Erinnerungen, op. cit, p. 63.

69 Gerhardine "Gerdy" Troost was born in Stuttgart on 3 March 1904. Member of the NSDAP since autumn 1932. For biography of Gerdy Troost, cf. the details contained in her denazification court file, Archives of the Bavarian State Munich, Denazification Court Box 1844 – Troost, Gerdy.

70 Proceedings of the denazification court pertaining to Mrs. Gerdy Troost, minutes of the session on 23 February 1950, sheet 158 (statement by the parties concerned). Archives of the Bavarian State, Munich, Denazification Court Box 1844 – Troost, Gerdy.

71 Draft letter by Gerdy Troost of 11 December 1934. Estate of Paul Ludwig Troost (Ana 325, Case 4), Bavarian State Library Munich, manuscript department.

[72] Leonhard Gall, born in Munich on 24 August 1884, had been employed as an architect by Paul Ludwig Troost since 1 July 1908. Training – according to his own statements – at technical colleges, then study visits to Italy and Belgium. Member of the NSDAP since 1 August 1932 (membership number 1274897). Cf. Munich City Archive mayor and council 1558 and the details contained in Gall's denazification court file, Archives of the Bavarian State, Munich, Denazification Court Box 482– Gall, Leonhard.

[73] Already in 1937 Gerdy Troost supervised the designing of the "Certificate of the Grand Cross of the Order of the German Eagle" that was awarded to Benito Mussolini – on the occasion of his state visit. Gerdy Troost commissioned the Munich-based graphic artist Franziska Kobell and Frieda Thiersch bookbinders with implementation; she worked with them on a fixed basis from 1939. Cf. estate of Paul Ludwig Troost (Ana 325, certificates), Bavarian State Library, manuscript department.

[74] Sophie Rützow, Betreuerin eines Vermächtnisses, in: Münchner Neueste Nachrichten, 25 July 1937. Munich City Archive, collection of newspaper clippings.

[75] I. v. W., Aus der Arbeit von Frau Professor Troost, in: Völkischer Beobachter, 15 July 1937.

[76] Albert Speer, Erinnerungen, op. cit, p. 63.

[77] ibid.

[78] Erich Walter Herbell to Lord Mayor OB Fiehler [25 May 1939]. Munich City Archive, culture department 602.

[79] Cf. Wolfram Selig, "Arisierung" in München. Die Vernichtung jüdischer Existenz 1937 – 1939, Berlin 2004, p. 809.

[80] The "Golden Party Badge" was awarded to members of the NSDAP with membership numbers 1 to 100,000 or for special services.

[81] Lawyer Curt Frhr. v. Stackelberg to the public prosecutor of Denazification Court I, Bad Reichenhall, 27 October 1947. Archives of the Bavarian State, Munich, Denazification Court Box 1844 – Troost, Gerdy.

[82] Prosecutor general Senger to retired permanent secretary Camillo Sachs, Munich, 2 March 1950. Archives of the Bavarian State, Munich, Denazification Court Box 1844 – Troost, Gerdy.

[83] Alongside Leonhard Gall, the "irreplaceable artists" also included architects Hermann Giesler, Wilhelm Kreis and Paul Schultze-Naumburg, sculptors Arno Breker, Fritz Klimsch, Georg Kolbe and Joseph Thorak, painters Hermann Gradl, Arthur Kampf, Willy Kriegel and Werner Peiner as well as six authors and three musicians.

[84] Press release of the German News Agency of 18 August 1944. Munich City Archive mayor and council 1558.

[85] Affidavit by sculptor Hans Panzer, Munich, 17 April 1946. Archives of the Bavarian State, Munich, Denazification Court Box 482 – Gall, Leonhard.

[86] Dr. G. St. [Georg Steinlein], Wiederbelebung des Münchener Bau- und Kunstlebens, in: Die Bauzeitung, 5 May 1933, p. 159.

[87] The Old Botanical Gardens were ultimately redesigned by Oswald Bieber und Josef Wackerle between 1935 and 1937 following plans bequeathed by Paul Ludwig Troost; this took the form of an ensemble of monumental fountain complex (Neptune Fountain), exhibition pavilion and coffee house (today's Park-Café).

[88] Cf. Karl Arndt, Das "Haus der Deutschen Kunst" – ein Symbol der neuen Machtverhältnisse, in: Nationalsozialismus und "Entartete Kunst". Die "Kunststadt" München 1937, ed. Peter-Klaus Schuster, Munich 1987, p. 71.

[89] Meeting of the city council on 26 April 1933. Munich City Archive, minutes of the city council.

[90] Dr. Bertha Antonia Walln to Bayerische Gartenbau-Gesellschaft e. V., 12 May 1933. Bavarian Administration of Palaces, Gardens and Lakes, 431 / 1 Rep. Reg. 75a No. 54.

[91] Memorandum of the Bavarian Administration of Palaces, Gardens and Lakes of 24 August 1933. Bavarian Administration of State-Owned Palaces, Gardens and Lakes, 431 / 1 Rep. Reg. 75a No. 54.

[92] Cf. in this context: Gerhard K.F. Stinglwagner, Von Mönchen, Prinzen und Ministern. Das Gebäude des Landwirtschaftsministeriums und seine Nachbarschaft, München 1991, p. 34 et seq. – I would like to thank Mr Klaus Bäumler for this bibliographical reference and important information on the urban development surrounding the "House of German Art".

[93] The new annexe was enlarged in horseshoe shape; furthermore, the inner courtyards was redesigned as a sky-lit hall. The interior was designed by the Troost Studio.

[94] Local building commission of the "Capital of the Movement" to Nana Merbitz, 1 July 1937. Munich City Archive, LBK 10240.

[95] House of German Art (New Glass Palace), Report for the Year 1939 [Munich 1940], p. 11. Historical Archive of Haus der Kunst, HdDK 18/1.

[96] Cf. Meeting of the councillors on 7 November 1940. Munich City Archive, minutes of the city council.

[97] Cf. Ulrike Haerendel, Die Zwangsveräußerung jüdischen Immobilienbesitzes, in: Angelika Baumann / Andreas Heusler, München arisiert. Entrechtung und Enteignung der Juden in der NS-Zeit, Munich 2004, p. 118 et seq.

[98] Wir danken dem Führer!, in: Völkischer Beobachter, 19 March 1936. Historical Archive of Haus der Kunst, HdDK 56 / 1.

[99] A. H. [Alexander Heilmeyer], Modell-Ausstellung im Hofgarten, in: Münchner Neueste Nachrichten, 22 July 1933. Historical Archive of Haus der Kunst, HdDK 54 / 1.

[100] Hans Kiener, Das neue Münchner Kunstausstellungsgebäude, in: Münchner Neueste Nachrichten, 16 July 1933. Historical Archive of Haus der Kunst, HdDK 54 / 1.

[101] Cf. Haus der Deutschen Kunst. Beginn der Bauarbeiten, in: Münchner Neueste Nachrichten, 27 November 1933 and: Beginn der Bauarbeiten für

das Haus der Deutschen Kunst, in: Völkischer Beobachter, 27 November 1933. Historical Archive of Haus der Kunst, HdDK 54 / 1.

102 Cf. the corresponding city council resolution of 11 May 1933. Munich City Archive, minutes of the city council.

103 Heinrich Kahl & Co. GmbH to the construction management of the House of German Art, 10 August 1934. Historical Archive of Haus der Kunst, HdDK 2 / B.

104 Roofing company / building tinsmith's shop Balthasar Dotterweich on the construction management of the House of German Art, 28 June 1934. Historical Archive of Haus der Kunst, HdDK 2 / D.

105 Cf. SS Oberführer and adjutant to State Minister H. Höflich to the construction management of the House of German Art, 18 January 1937. Historical Archive of Haus der Kunst, HdDK 2 / M.

106 Cf. catalogue of services and directory of firms of the House of German Art, compiled on 21 January 1939. Historical Archive of Haus der Kunst, HdDK 14.

107 Quoted in: Michael Backmund, Baufirma Leonhard Moll, in: Ort und Erinnerung. Nationalsozialismus in München, ed. Winfried Nerdinger, Salzburg 2006, p. 117.

108 [fw.], Ein Riesenpfahlbau der Gegenwart. An der Baustellung in der Prinzregentenstrasse, in: Völkischer Beobachter, 26 June 1936. Historical Archive of Haus der Kunst, HdDK 54 / 1.

109 Alexander Heilmeyer, Das junge Deutschland baut seiner Kunst ein eigen Haus, in: Die Kunst im Dritten Reich, July / August 1937, p. 15.

110 Das "Haus der Deutschen Kunst" in München – ein Bau im "Deutschen Stil"! in: Münchner Illustrierte Presse, No. 3 / 1936. Historical Archive of Haus der Kunst, HdDK 56 / 1.

111 Cf. Karl Arndt, Das "Haus der Deutschen Kunst", op. cit., p. 75.

112 Due to this trivial recourse to classicistic elements of form, critical contemporaries – especially after 1945 – have given the building the epithet "Temple to White Sausages" or "Athens Goods Station".

113 Alexander Heilmeyer, Das junge Deutschland baut seiner Kunst ein eigen Haus, op. cit., p. 17.

114 In contrast to the building actually implemented, the model exhibited in July 1933 had – in addition to the "national emblem" mounted above the main portal – also statues between the columns of the portico and an inscription – not specified in any more detail – on the architrave.

115 Cf. for this the comments in Section 3.3.

116 Goebbels Reden, 1932–1939, Vol. 1, ed. Helmut Heiber, Munich 1971, p. 91.

117 Alexander Heilmeyer, Das junge Deutschland baut seiner Kunst ein eigen Haus, op. cit., p. 17.

118 House of German Art (New Glass Palace) to the Administration of State-Owned Palaces, Gardens and Lakes, 9 September 1936. Bavarian Admin-

istration of State-Owned Palaces, Gardens and Lakes, 431 / 1 Rep. Reg. 75a No. 54.

119 Cf. Alexander Heilmeyer, Zu den Werken von Karl Heinz Dallinger, in: Die Kunst im Dritten Reich, Issue 10 (October 1938), p. 314 et seq. – In 2003, the murals that had up to that point been covered over with plywood panels were uncovered and restored as part of the "Critical Reconstruction" project.

120 These were the word used, for instance, by Gauleiter and Minister of the Interior Adolf Wagner in the foreword to the official exhibition catalogue for the "Great German Art Exhibition" in 1937.

121 Dieter Bartetzko, Obsession aus Stein. Die Architekten des "Dritten Reichs", in: Hitlers Künstler. Die Kultur im Dienst des Nationalsozialismus, ed. Hans Sarkowicz, Frankfurt a. M. / Leipzig 2004, p. 116.

122 Martin Broszat, Der Despot von München, in: Süddeutsche Zeitung, 30/ 31 March 1985. – In 1935, following the death of Hans Schemm, the Bavarian Minister of Education and the Arts, Adolf Wagner assumed the former's office. Wagner suffered a stroke in 1942 and died in Munich two years later. He was buried to the east of the northern "Temple of Honour" at Königsplatz.

123 Hans Joachim Hecker, Missbrauchtes Mäzenatentum? Die Gründung der Anstalt des öffentlichen Rechts "Haus der Deutschen Kunst (Neuer Glaspalast)" im Jahre 1933, in: Nationalsozialismus und "Entartete Kunst", op. cit., p. 57.

124 Adolf Wagner to Reich governor Ritter von Epp, 10 June 1933. Archives of the Bavarian State, Reich governor 668.

125 Cf. in this context – and specifically on Friedrich Doehlemann's career – Hans Joachim Hecker, Missbrauchtes Mäzenatentum? op. cit.

126 Statutes of the "House of German Art (New Glass Palace)". Corporation established under public law in Munich. Historical Archive of Haus der Kunst, HdDK 17.

127 Wording of a note written by August von Finck on 15 October 1974 in which he, among other things, emphasises that his involvement in the "House of German Art" only came about because, for various reasons, it seemed inopportune to make enemies of the new regime in 1933 by declining. – I would like to thank Dr. Heribald Närger and Chris Dercon for letting me use this document.

128 Cf. Karl Arndt, Das "Haus der Deutschen Kunst", op. cit., p. 63.

129 Helft mit am Bau des Hauses der deutschen Kunst! Ein Aufruf an das ganze deutsche Volk, in: Völkischer Beobachter, 18 July 1933. Historical Archive of Haus der Kunst, HdDK 54 / 1. – Virtually all of the organs of the press, which had already been brought in line with party policy, printed this appeal mid-July 1933.

130 According to a list contained in Haus der Kunst's archive, the total amount of all contributions came to 10,327,995.62 Reichsmarks. Historical Archive of Haus der Kunst, DIR 5 / 5.

131 Cf. duplicate of the transfer agreement of 22 June 1934. Historical Archive of Haus der Kunst, HdDK 5 / 1.

132 Meeting of the council of ministers on 29 August 1933. Archives of the Bavarian State, Reich governor 165.

133 Cf. 400 000 für das neue Kunstausstellungsgebäude, in: Münchner Neueste Nachrichten, 27 April 1933. Historical Archive of Haus der Kunst, HdDK 54/1.

134 House of German Art (New Glass Palace) to Deutsche Gesellschaft für öffentliche Arbeiten, 26 February 1934. Federal Archives Koblenz, R2 / 18722. – According to the Law on Reducing Unemployment, the terms of the load covered every restriction relating to the hiring of skilled workers and working hours.

135 Cf. the corresponding agreements contained in the inventory of the Historical Archive of Haus der Kunst, HdDK 23. – The free supplies of electricity were terminated after 1945.

136 As a rule, the foundation stone donors financed the construction of the "House of German Art" with 100,000 Reichsmarks each.

137 "Das ganze Volk nimmt Teil am Bau", in: Völkischer Beobachter, 25 May 1934. Historical Archive of Haus der Kunst, HdDK 56 / 1.

138 Unless stated otherwise, the brief biographies of the foundation stone donors were based on the information contained in the following sources: Deutsches Biographisches Archiv, Neue Deutsche Biographie (new issue), Munzinger Archiv.

139 Cf. Thomas Ramge, Die Flicks. Eine deutsche Familiengeschichte über Geld, Macht und Politik, Frankfurt am Main 2004, p. 79–145.

140 Thomas Rother, Die Krupps. Durch fünf Generationen Stahl, Frankfurt am Main 2001, p. 45.

141 Institut für Zeitgeschichte, MA 292.

142 Cf. Henry Ashby Turner, General Motors und die Nazis. Das Ringen um Opel, Berlin 2006.

143 For information on Böttcherstrasse cf. Arn Stromeyer, Parsifal in Bremen. Richard Wagner, Ludwig Roselius und die Böttcherstraße, Weimar 2002.

144 Cf. Die ungeliebte Republik, Dokumente zur Innen- und Außenpolitik Weimars 1918–1933, ed. Wolfgang Michalka / Gottfried Niedhart, Munich 1980, p. 340 et seq.

145 Cf. the correspondence between Karl Astel and Heinrich Himmler dating from the year 1935. Institut für Zeitgeschichte, MA 297.

146 Volker Koop, Das Schmutzige Vermögen. Das Dritte Reich, die I. G. Farben und die Schweiz, München 2005, p. 13.

147 Cf. 150 Jahre Geschäfte des Siemens-Konzerns. Geschäfte in finsteren Zeiten, published by isw sozial-ökologische Wirtschaftsforschung München e. V., Munich 1997, p. 8–11.

148 Adolf Hitler, Mein Kampf, Munich 1939 (489th – 493th edition), p. 139.

149 The protest letter was published in Münchner Neueste Nachrichten on

16/17 April. Replicated in: Hartmut Zelinsky, Richard Wagner. Ein deutsches Thema, Berlin / Vienna 1983, p. 195.

150 Münchens Sendung für die deutsche Kunst. Aufruf zum "Tag der Deutschen Kunst" am 14. und 15. Oktober 1933, in: Münchner Neueste Nachrichten, 18 September 1933. Historical Archive of Haus der Kunst, HdDK 54 / 2.

151 Tag der Deutschen Kunst. Gegen die Ewiggestrigen, in: Münchner Neueste Nachrichten, 28 September 1933. Historical Archive of Haus der Kunst, HdDK 54/2.

152 Cf. Im Blickpunkt der künstlerischen Welt, in: Münchner Neueste Nachrichten, 3 October 1933. Historical Archive of Haus der Kunst, HdDK 54/2.

153 Cf. meeting of the budget committee of the City of Munich on 17 November 1933. Munich City Archive, minutes of the city council.

154 Richard Klein was additionally appointed director of the Munich Academy of Applied Art in 1935.

155 a. h. [Alexander Heilmeyer], Die Künstler bei der Arbeit, in: Münchner Neueste Nachrichten, 7 October 1933. Historical Archive of Haus der Kunst, HdDK 54/2.

156 Cf. The Temple of German Art Munich, ed. Karl Drechsler, Munich 1933.

157 The Künstlerhaus at Lenbachplatz was built between 1892 and 1900, according to plans by Gabriel von Seidl, as a club house for Munich's artist community. In the course of the formation of "Kameradschaft der Künstler" in July 1938 and the associated dissolution of the artists' associations, the Künstlerhaus was transferred to the ownership of the Kameradschaft as "a present from the Führer". The building burnt to the ground in July 1944 following an air raid. The newly reconstructed Künstlerhaus was reopened in 1961.

158 Tag der Deutschen Kunst, in: Münchner Neueste Nachrichten, 9 October 1933. Historical Archive of Haus der Kunst, HdDK 54/2.

159 München rüstet zum Tag der Deutschen Kunst, in: Münchner Neueste Nachrichten, 15 September 1933. Historical Archive of Haus der Kunst, HdDK 54/2.

160 Quoted in: Adolf Hitler, Reden zur Kunst- und Kulturpolitik, ed. Robert Eickmeyer, Frankfurt am Main 2004, p. 57 et seq.

161 Josef Wackerle, in turn, commissioned numerous artists associated with the Munich Academy with fitting out the groups and festive carriages designed by him. The costumes were drawn by Professors Leo Pasetti and Julius Heß. Organisational direction was assumed by painter Konrad Hommel, who immediately rose to Hitler's favourite portrait painter. – With regards to the iconography, cf. Stefan Schweizer, "Glanzzeiten deutscher Kultur". Der historische Festzug zur Grundsteinlegung des "Hauses der Deutschen Kunst" 1933 in München, in: Tel Aviver Jahrbuch für Deutsche Geschichte 2006, ed. Moshe Zuckermann, Göttingen 2006, p. 192 et seq.

162 Grundsteinlegung des Hauses der Deutschen Kunst, published by the

Munich Upper Bavaria Gauleiter's office of the NSDAP, Munich 1933, p.32.

163 Tag der Deutschen Kunst 1937, in: Münchner Stadtanzeiger, 3 June 1937.

164 Cf. Sie alle halfen mit, in: Münchner Neueste Nachrichten, 25 July 1937.

165 This included the celebrations on the occasion of the 9 November, the annual "celebration of the foundation of the party" on 24 February as well as state receptions and state funerals.

166 Cf. Erlebnis, nicht nur Schau. Der Festzug am Tag der Deutschen Kunst "Zweitausend Jahre deutscher Kultur", in: Münchner Stadtanzeiger, 11 June 1937.

167 Josef Wackerle is alleged to have – as he had communicated through his lawyer in 1946 – declined the commission as the 1937 procession was subject to party influence even from an artistic perspective. Cf. Michael Hermann, "2000 Jahre deutsche Kultur" – historische Festzüge im nationalsozialistischen München, in: Zeitschrift für bayerische Landesgeschichte, 1997 / issue 2, p. 367. – Wackerle had been appointed by Goebbels to the presidential council of the Reich Chamber of Fine Arts in 1936 and was a sought-after artist for the duration of the Nazi period; he designed, for example, the fountain complex (Neptune Fountain) in the redesigned Old Botanical Gardens.

168 Kaspar and Klein were relieved of their offices by the military government in 1945; Hermann Kaspar was, however, able to return to his professorship as early as November 1946. Cf. Reinhard Müller-Mehlis, Der Fall Hermann Kaspar. Eine Dokumentation, Munich, no date [1966].

169 Dr. G. St. [Georg Steinlein], Das künstlerische München, in: Die Bauzeitung, 15 December 1933.

170 Cf. Michael Hermann, "2000 Jahre deutsche Kultur", loc. cit

171 "Der Tag der Deutschen Kunst als Arbeitgeber", in: Münchener Beobachter, 18 December 1937. Historical Archive of Haus der Kunst, HdDK 54 / 2.

172 For instance, a trip to Lake Starnberg and Ammersee were on offer, which had a programme including a visit to the "Führer's cell" in the prison at Landsberg am Lech. Cf. Tag der Deutschen Kunst München 1937, published by the Directorate of the Day of German Art, Munich 1937, p. 24.

173 Deutschland-Berichte der Sozialdemokratischen Partei Deutschlands (Sopade), Fourth Volume (1937), Salzhausen / Frankfurt am Main 1989, p. 1075 et seq.

174 Zweitausend Jahre Deutsche Kultur. Der Festzug am Tag der Deutschen Kunst 1937 zu München, published by the Directorate of the Day of German Art, Munich 1937, p. 24.

175 The procession started in Prinzregentenstrasse, from there it led past the "House of German Art", through Von-der-Tannstrasse, in the direction of Siegestor. At the university, the procession turned in the direction of Odeonsplatz and marched on to Königsplatz. The next stations took it through Lenbachplatz, Karlsplatz and Marienplatz to Maximilianstrasse, where

the procession dissolved at the Maxmonument. As of 1938, the procession turned off from the "House of German Art" into Königinstrasse and went over Ohmstrasse to Leopoldstrasse and from there through the Siegestor.

176 Exhibition Catalogue München – "Hauptstadt der Bewegung«, op. cit., Munich 2002, p. 342.

177 Festzug "2000 Jahre deutsche Kultur", in: Völkischer Beobachter, 20 July 1937. Historical Archive of Haus der Kunst, HdDK 54 / 2.

178 Vom Plan zur glanzvollen Wirklichkeit, in: Münchner Neueste Nachrichten, 19 June 1938.

179 Cf. Mitwirkende gesucht, in: Münchner Stadtanzeiger, 2 July 1939.

180 ibid.

181 Quoted in: Robert S. Wistrich, Ein Wochenende in München. Kunst, Propaganda und Terror im Dritten Reich, Munich 1996, p. 93.

182 Isabel Hilton, Filming Hitler: July 1939, in: The Independent on Sunday, 16 May 1993. German translation quoted in: Robert S. Wistrich, Ein Wochenende in München, op. cit., p. 89.

183 Lebendiges Bekenntnis zur Kunst im Krieg. Die Große Deutsche Kunstausstellung 1940, in: Münchner Neueste Nachrichten, 27 July 1940.

184 The "Day of German Art" was financed by subsidies from the City of Munich, the State of Bavaria and the Propaganda Ministry, as well as a donation from Adolf Hitler of 500,000 Reichsmarks. However, these amounts were insufficient by far to cover the costs incurred – 3.8 million Reichsmarks were needed in 1938 alone. The amount of funds that had to be raised to cover the costs of the procession "2000 Years of German Culture" is not known. According to an estimate from 1939, the groups "Ostmark" and "Sudetenland" caused expenses of 110,000 and 190,000 Reichsmarks, respectively – cf. conference on the financing of large-scale events in Munich, 18 November 1940. Archives of the Bavarian State, Munich, NSDAP 101 Also: Michael Hermann, "2000 Jahre deutsche Kultur", op. cit., p. 376 et seq.

185 Conference on the financing of large-scale events in Munich (continuation of the conference on 18 November 1940), Archives of the Bavarian State, Munich, NSDAP 101.

186 Große Deutsche Kunstausstellung 1937 im Haus der Deutschen Kunst zu München. Official Exhibition Catalogue, Munich 1937, p. 5.

187 Großtaten deutschen Aufbauwillens. Der Führer beim Richtfest zum Haus der Deutschen Kunst, in: Münchner Neueste Nachrichten, 1 July 1935. Historical Archive of Haus der Kunst, HdDK 54/10.

188 Cf. Paul Ortwin Rave, Kunstdiktatur im Dritten Reich (1949), new ed. Uwe M. Schneede, Berlin [1987], p. 99. – This exhibition proposed by the general director of the Bavarian State Painting Collection, Ernst Buchner, was to be designed along the lines of the famous annual exhibition of 1906 by the National Gallery.

189 House of German Art (New Glass Palace), Report for the Year 1936 [Munich 1937], p. 14. Historical Archive of Haus der Kunst, HdDK 18/1.

[190] Official letter from the "House of German Art (New Glass Palace)" to German artists, November 1936, replicated in: Nationalsozialismus und "Entartete Kunst", op. cit., p. 258.

[191] Ausstellung 1937 im Haus der Deutschen Kunst, in: Münchner Neueste Nachrichten, 15 January 1937. Historical Archive of Haus der Kunst, HdDK 54/1.

[192] According to the exhibition terms, the artists set the sales prices themselves. In the event of a sale, ten percent went to the exhibition management of the "House of German Art" as commission. Cf. for this, the comments in Section 6.2

[193] By the end of 1936, according to Paul Ortwin Rave, 14,300 painters, 2,900 sculptors and 4,200 commercial artists belonged to the Reich Chamber of Fine Arts formed in 1933. cf. Paul Ortwin Rave, Kunstdiktatur im Dritten Reich (1949), new ed. Uwe M. Schneede, loc. cit., op. cit., p. 93. – 5000 painters lived in Munich alone. Cf. Joseph Wulf, Die Bildenden Künste im Dritten Reich, Gütersloh 1963, p. 109.

[194] Quoted in: Gisela Kleine, Gabriele Münter und Wassily Kandinsky. Biographie eines Paares, Munich 1993, p. 627.

[195] ibid. p. 775, note 69. – All four paintings submitted by Gabriele Münter to the "Great German Art Exhibition" were rejected. The artist did not apply another time.

[196] Die Tagebücher von Joseph Goebbels. Sämtliche Fragmente, ed. Elke Fröhlich, Part 1 / Vol. 3, Munich 1987, p. 167.

[197] Lynn H. Nicholas, Der Raub der Europa. Das Schicksal europäischer Kunstwerke im Dritten Reich, Munich 1997, p. 27.

[198] Die Tagebücher von Joseph Goebbels, op. cit., p. 181.

[199] ibid. p. 200.

[200] For Heinrich Hoffmann's career, cf. Rudolf Herz, Hoffmann & Hitler, Munich 1994, p. 26 et seq.

[201] Cf. Große Deutsche Kunstausstellung 1937 im Haus der Deutschen Kunst zu München loc. cit. – For art in the "Third Reich" cf. Berthold Hinz, Die Malerei im deutschen Faschismus, Munich 1974 and Klaus Wolbert, Die Nackten und die Toten des "Dritten Reichs", Gießen 1982.

[202] Der Führer weiht das Haus der Deutschen Kunst, in: Münchner Neueste Nachrichten, 19 July 1937.

[203] Winfried Nerdinger, Fatale Kontinuität: Akademiegeschichte von den zwanziger bis zu den fünfziger Jahren, in: Tradition und Widerspruch. 175 Jahre Kunstakademie München, ed. Thomas Zacharias, Munich 1985, p. 191 et seq.

[204] Fritz Alexander Kauffmann, Die neue deutsche Malerei, Berlin 1941, p. 130.

[205] Adolf Hitler weiht das Haus der Deutschen Kunst, in: Völkischer Beobachter, 19 July 1937. Historical Archive of Haus der Kunst, HdDK 54 / 13.

[206] Speech printed in: Haus der Kunst 1937–1997. Ein historische Dokumentation, edited by Sabine Brantl, Munich [1997], p. 74 et seq.

[207] John Heartfield, Der Schnitt entlang der Zeit. Selbstzeugnisse, Erinnerungen, Interpretationen, ed. Roland März, Dresden 1981, p. 390.

[208] The term "degenerate art" was originally coined by the Jewish writer Max Nordau (1849–1923) who designated European art in its entirety as decadent and unhealthy in his book "Degeneracy" that was published in 1892/93. National Socialist art writers such as Paul Schultze-Naumburg and Wolfgang Willrich appropriated this description for their devastating discourses on modern art. Musicians and composers who were not approved by the Reich were also defamed as "degenerate". Consequently, there was also a travelling exhibition by the name of "degenerate music" that was staged in 1938 that pilloried portraits and the works of undesired composers.

[209] Speech printed in: Adolf Hitler, Reden zur Kunst- und Kulturpolitik op. cit., p. 811 et seq. – This meant a final rejection of the attempt, advocated by Goebbels, to make "nordic" expressionism acceptable to the Third Reich.

[210] Cf. Christoph Zuschlag, "Entartete Kunst". Ausstellungsstrategien im Nazi-Deutschland, Worms 1993, p. 146 et seq. and Mario-Andreas von Lüttichau, "Deutsche Kunst" und "Entartete Kunst". Die Münchner Ausstellungen 1937, in: Nationalsozialismus und "Entartete Kunst", op. cit., p. 94 et seq.

[211] Entartete Kunst am Pranger, in: Völkischer Beobachter, 20 July 1937.

[212] Wolfgang Willrich, Die Säuberung des Kunsttempels. Eine kunstpolitische Kampfschrift zur Gesundung deutscher Kunst im nordischen Geist, Munich/ Berlin 1937. – The preamble to the book reads: "May this book help those who understand 'art' to be something noble, healthy, a natural expression of life from nation and kind, for nation and kind ... May it be a weapon in the hands of the fighters for the liberation of the German character from rubbish and filth and unhealthy spirit." The document mainly consisted of pictures and quotes from art historians, critics and artists stigmatised as "degenerate", commented on by the author following the purpose laid down in the mentioned preamble.

[213] Quoted in: Otto Thomae, Die Propaganda-Maschinerie. Bildende Kunst und Öffentlichkeitsarbeit im Dritten Reich, Berlin 1978, p. 40.

[214] The two sculptures were secured from Böhmer's art store in Güstrow in 1947 and handed over to the National Gallery in East Berlin two years later.

[215] Paul Ortwin Rave, Kunstdiktatur im Dritten Reich, op. cit., p. 104 et seq.

[216] Christoph Zuschlag, "Entartete Kunst", op. cit., p. 178.

[217] ibid. p. 178 (Document 18).

[218] Die Tagebücher von Joseph Goebbels, op. cit., p. 192.

[219] Cf. Zuschlag, "Entartete Kunst", op. cit. p. 352.

[220] Paul Ortwin Rave, Kunstdiktatur im Dritten Reich, op. cit., p. 143 et seq.

[221] Die Tagebücher von Joseph Goebbels, op. cit., p. 204.

222 Speech printed in: Nationalsozialismus und "Entartete Kunst", op. cit., p. 217 et seq.

223 The text read: "Tortured canvas – spiritual decay – morbid fantasies – mentally ill bunglers, awarded prizes by coteries of Jews, praised by literary figures, were the products and producers of an 'art' on which state and municipal institutions wasted millions from the German national wealth, without batting an eyelid, while German artists went hungry at the same time. The 'art' was of the same nature as the 'state' that produced it. Just have a look at it! Judge for yourselves! Visit the 'degenerate art' exhibition – Hofgarten-Arkaden, Galeriestrasse 4 – entrance free – forbidden for young people"

224 Deutschland-Berichte der Sozialdemokratischen Partei Deutschlands (Sopade), Fourth Volume (1937), op. cit., p. 1534 et seq.

225 Cf. Joseph Wulf, Die bildenden Künste im Dritten Reich, op. cit., p. 363.

226 Cf. in this context the corresponding entries in the diaries of Joseph Goebbels, who had also initiated this action. Die Tagebücher von Joseph Goebbels, op. cit., p. 211 et seq.

227 Cf. Lynn H. Nicholas, Der Raub der Europa, op. cit., p. 35 et seq.

228 The works on offer at the auction included, for example, Vincent van Gogh's Self- Portrait (1888) from the inventory of the Bavarian State Painting Collections, now located in the Fogg Art Museum in Cambridge. Cf. for this: Stephanie Barron, Die Auktion in der Galerie Fischer, in: "Entartete Kunst". Das Schicksal der Avantgarde im Nazi-Deutschland, ed. Stephanie Barron, Munich 1992, p. 135 et seq.

229 Staatsgalerie moderner Kunst München. Ein Rundgang durch die Sammlung, Munich 1987, p. 109 et seq. – The collection includes paintings and works on paper by Max Beckmann, Otto Dix, Oskar Kokoschka, Franz Marc and Egon Schiele.

230 Cf. Diether Schmidt, Schriften deutscher Künstler des 20. Jahrhunderts, Vol. II, Dresden 1964, p. 252.

231 Cf. Lynn H. Nicholas, Der Raub der Europa, op. cit., p. 39.

232 Cf. Künftig zwei Ausstellungen im Jahr, in: Münchner Neueste Nachrichten, 17 July 1937.

233 Cf. Architektur und Kunsthandwerk, in: Münchner Zeitung, 27/28 November 1937. Historical Archive of Haus der Kunst, HdDK 54 / 14.

234 Cf. Architektur und Kunsthandwerk, in: Münchner Neueste Nachrichten, 27 November 1937. Historical Archive of Haus der Kunst, HdDK 54 / 14.

235 ibid., p. 37. – The sales proceeds came to 73,300 Reichsmarks.

236 Cf. Im Dezember Eröffnung. Die zweite deutsche Architektur- und Kunsthandwerk-Austellung, undated newspaper clipping. Historical Archive of Haus der Kunst, HdDK 54 / 14.

237 Report on the 1939 Annual Meeting, in: House of German Art. Report for the Year 1939, [Munich 1940], p. 9.

238 Cf. number of visitors to the "Second German Architecture and Handi-

craft Exhibition 1938 / 39", Historical Archive of Haus der Kunst, HdDK 32 / 5.

239 Quoted in House of German Art . Report for the Year 1938 [Munich 1939], p. 23.

240 This decree was revoked for a short period following the armistice with France in June 1940 and led to resumption of the building work on the so-called "Führer cities".

241 Cf. Otto Thomae, Die Propaganda-Maschinerie. Bildende Kunst und Öffentlichkeitsarbeit im Dritten Reich, op. cit., p. 69.

242 Cf. for this, Section 3.1 in this book.

243 Karl-Heinz Meißner, "München ist ein heißer Boden. Aber wir gewinnen ihn allmählich doch." Münchner Akademien, Galerien und Museen im Ausstellungsjahr 1937, in: Nationalsozialismus und "Entartete Kunst", op. cit., p. 44.

244 Henry Picker, Hitlers Tischgespräche im Führerhauptquartier, Augsburg 1963, p. 213 [27 March 1942].

245 "Große Deutsche Kunstausstellung 1940". Erfahrungen in Bezug auf das Hängen und Stellen der Arbeiten, 23 July 1940 (typescript). Historical Archive of Haus der Kunst, HdDK 35 / 6. "No 'modern' pictures; the following, among others, removed at Führer's request: Beutner Johannes, Dresden (female nudes), Clarenbach Max, Wittlaer, Dörfel Otto, Munich (female nudes), Dörffel Heinz, Leipzig (lithographies), Doll Franz, Munich, Freytag Otto, Berlin (draft mural), Harrach Hans-Albrecht, Graf, Munich (female nudes), Hempfing Wilhelm, Karlsruhe (lying female nude), Hergarde Bernhard, Düsseldorf, Lautenbacher Hias, Kochel (Thorak apprentice), Lenzner Erika, Berlin, Maxon Wilhelm G., Munich (watercolours), Miller-Diflo Otto, Munich, Moroder Siegfried, Munich (terracotta works), Müller Erich Martin, Berlin (bathing boys), Müller Georg, Munich (female figure), Müller-Oerlinghausen Berthold, Berlin (small bronze statue), Nuß Fritz, Stuttgart (female nudes), Pieper Josef, Düsseldorf, Poetzelberger Oswald, Munich, Protzen Carl Theodor, Munich, Reiß-Schmidt Ernst, Düsseldorf and Reiß-Schmidt Helwig, Düsseldorf (small sculptures), Reusing Fritz, Düsseldorf, Ruhmer Helmut, Florence, Schmurr Wilhelm, Düsseldorf, Schramm-Zittau Rudolf, Dresden, Spethmann Albert, Bad Tölz, Zügel Heinrich von, Munich.

246 ibid.

247 Cf. the corresponding entries in the account books. Historical Archive of Haus der Kunst, HdDK 24 / 1-6. – A large portion of the information from the accounts receivable and the accounts payable of the "Haus der Deutschen Kunst" have also been accessible at www.gdk-research.de since 2011. This online database was developed by the Zentralinstitut für Kunstgeschichte, Munich, the Deutsches Historisches Museum and Haus der Kunst in 2010/11.

248 ibid.

249 The painting was delivered to the Führer Building in Munich's Arcisstrasse

in 1942 and confiscated by the Americans after the war. Until 1998 it was stored at the Higher Financial Directorate of the City of Munich; now it belongs to the inventory of the Deutsches Historisches Museum in Berlin.

250 The total cost of the works purchased in 1938 came to 47,577.70 Reichsmarks and was paid for by the Reich chancery. Cf. entry for Adolf Hitler in the accounts receivable for the year 1938, Historical Archive of Haus der Kunst, HdDK 24 / 2.

251 Cf. "Deposit Ledger for Pictures", Historical Archive of Haus der Kunst, HdDK 45 / 1.

252 Die Tagebücher von Joseph Goebbels, op. cit., p. 205.

253 Historical Archive of Haus der Kunst, HdDK 34 / 2.

254 A total of 2,538 artists took part in the eight "Great German Art Exhibitions". The file of artists extant in Haus der Kunst's archive, which recorded all submissions from 1938 onwards, contains some 7,000 file cards. Cf. Historical Archive of Haus der Kunst, HdDK 36 / 1-6 and 37/1-2.

255 Cf. Christoph Becker / Annette Lagler, Biennale Venedig. Der deutsche Beitrag 1895–1995, Stuttgart 1995, p. 142 et seq.

256 Die Tagebücher von Joseph Goebbels, op. cit., p. 369.

257 Arno Breker, Im Strahlungsfeld der Erinnerungen, Preussisch Oldendorf 1972, p. 100.

258 Cf. Otto Thomae, Die Propaganda-Maschinerie, op. cit., p. 440.

259 ibid. p.326.

260 State Ministry for Teaching and Cultural Affairs to the Munich Academy of Fine Arts, 10 November 1938. Archives of the Bavarian State, MK 40917.

261 Academy of Fine Arts to the State Ministry for Teaching and Cultural Affairs, 7 July 1937. Archives of the Bavarian State, MK 40901.

262 Cf. Wolfgang Kehr, Aus der Chronik der Münchner Akademie der Bildenden Künste: Direktoren bzw. Präsidenten, Professoren, ordentliche Professoren, Ereignisse, in: Tradition und Widerspruch, op. cit., p. 318.

263 Federal Archives Berlin, R43 / 3575f. 38–48. Also: Otto Thomae, Die Propaganda-Maschinerie, op. cit., p. 390ff.

264 Cf. Volker Dahm, Künstler als Funktionäre. Das Propagandaministerium und die Reichskulturkammer, in: Hitlers Künstler, op. cit., p. 107.

265 Cf. file of employees/salaried staff of the "House of German Art". Historical Archive of Haus der Kunst, HdDK 36 / 2.

266 Cf. the corresponding employee records for the period from 1936 to 1945. Historical Archive of Haus der Kunst, HdDK 20 / A–Z.

267 For example, according to the details contained in the employees' card files, 18 of a total of 56 members of staff who were employed at the House of German Art until 31 December 1940, were members of the NSDAP. Three employees did not give any details in this respect.

268 Karl Kolb was born in Munich on 14 October 1894. Member of the NSDAP since 1937. With regard to his professional career, Karl Kolb made

the following statement in April 1946: "I lost my livelihood through the Hitler regime in 1933 through no fault of my own and joined the NSDAP, under pressure as can be proven, to avoid an impending renewed loss of my livelihood in 1937." In summary proceedings by the denazification court in 1948, he was classified as a "follower" and sentenced to a financial penalty of 1,800 Reichsmarks. Cf. denazification court file for Karl Kolb, Archives of the Bavarian State, Munich, Denazification Court Box 929 – Kolb, Karl.

269 House of German Art . Report for the Year 1935 [Munich 1936], p. 7. – At this point, the offices of the "House of German Art" were located at Maximiliansplatz 22 / 3.

270 Cf. for example the catalogue of measures relating to the design of the "Great German Art Exhibition 1939". Historical Archive of Haus der Kunst, HdDK 35 / 2.

271 Confirmation dated 23 September 1941. Historical Archive of Haus der Kunst, HdDK 35 / 17.

272 Cf. details contained in hand-written CV of Ottmar Endres, 5 October 1936. Historical Archive of Haus der Kunst, HdDK 20 / E. – Ottmar Endres was born in Munich on 19 June 1910. He was a member of the SA from 1933 to 1937, he joined the Nazi cultural association in 1936. Member of the NSDAP since 1937. In 1942, the Hitler Youth leadership awarded him the rank of cadre unit leader on account of his "specialist artistic knowledge". In 1948, Ottmar Endres was classified by the denazification court as a "follower" and sentenced to a financial penalty of 1,000 Reichsmarks. Cf. denazification court file for Ottmar Endres, Archives of the Bavarian State, Munich, Denazification Court Box 360 – Endres, Ottmar.

273 Mitteilungsblatt der NS-Kulturgemeinde "zur Unterrichtung der Urkunden- und Buchausstellung 'Wehrhaftes Deutschland – Kampf um das Reich'", 14 to 19 June 1936. Historical Archive of Haus der Kunst, HdDK 20 / E.

274 Prof. H.R. Rosemann, Darmstadt Technical University, to the "House of German Art (New Glass Palace)", Darmstadt, 26 October 1936. Historical Archive of Haus der Kunst, HdDK 20 / E.

275 Several issues of the official exhibition catalogue were published for each "Great German Art Exhibition" and were available for the price of one Reichsmark.

276 Cf. for this, the catalogue of measures drafted by Karl Kolb relating to the replacement of works of art during the "Great German Art Exhibition 1943". Historical Archive of Haus der Kunst, HdDK 35 / 16.

277 That year, a total of 1,753 works were exhibited.

278 Cf. overview of numbers of visitors. Archives of the Bavarian State, HdDtK 156. Also: Historical Archive of Haus der Kunst, HdDK 32 / 1–7.

279 Cf. for this the accounts receivable in which all buyers and their purchases were recorded from 1938 onwards. Historical Archive of Haus der Kunst, HdDK 24.

280 Meldungen aus dem Reich. Die geheimen Lageberichte des Sicherheits-

dienstes der SS 1938–1945, Vol. 1–17, ed. Heinz Boberach, Herrsching 1984. Here: Vol 5, p. 1485 and Vol. 9, p. 3,397.

281 Adjutancy of the German army to the House of German Art, 25 January 1942. Historical Archive of Haus der Kunst, HdDK 50.

282 Reich Ministry for Popular Enlightenment and Propaganda to the House of German Art, 5 February 1945. Historical Archive, HdDK 50.

283 As note 278. As late as in December 1944, paintings were rehung and works sold were replaced with new works that had remained in the store until that point.

284 Sale of the oil painting "Heller Tag" ["Bright Day"] by Josef Steib (catalogue number A397) to a private buyer from Gräfelfing for a price of 5,000 Reichsmarks. Archives of the Bavarian State, HdDtK 18.

285 Cf. notes 266, 268 and 272.

286 Cf. The House of German Art Processing Centre to Arno Breker. Historical Archive of Haus der Kunst, HdDK 53 / 1.

287 The works were seized by the US military government on the basis of "Allied Control Authority Directive No. 30 (confiscation of national socialist and militaristic art)".

288 The House of German Art Processing Centre to Arno Breker, 6 November 1948. Historical Archive of Haus der Kunst, HdDK 53 / 4.

289 Cf. the documentation edited by Monika Flacke "Bilder aus NS-Reichsbesitz. Ankäufe aus den 'Großen Deutschen Kunstausstellungen'", Berlin 1999 (Deutsches Historisches Museum, CD-ROM I).

290 Thomas Wimmer und sein München, Munich 1989, p. 35.

291 Cf. minutes of the second meeting on camouflage as air-raid protection of the House of German Art, 26 September 1942. Historical Archive of Haus der Kunst, HdDK 15. – August von Finck, Karl Kolb, Leonhard Gall and representatives of the district air commands and the structural engineering office took part in the meeting, among others.

292 Confiscation took place under the legal title of "institution that served as a tool of the political regime". Cf. Interview with Minister of Education and the arts, in: Abendzeitung, 9/10 July 1960.

293 Peter A. Ade, Picasso, Kokoschka und all die anderen ... Meine abenteuerlichen Jahre für die Kunst, Munich 2001.

294 Jella Lepmann, Die Kinderbuchbrücke, Frankfurt a. M. 1964, p. 64.

295 The Munich American, 16 June 1950.

296 Some 200 civilian members of staff were employed each year for kitchen and cleaning work. cf. Historical Archive of Haus der Kunst, OMGB 5.

297 Peter A. Ade, Picasso, Kokoschka und all die anderen, op. cit., p. 22.

298 Cf. Gavriel D. Rosenfeld, Architektur und Gedächtnis, Munich 2004, p. 160.

299 Aus dem Rathaus, in: Abendzeitung, 17 September 1948.

300 Bayerische Staatsgemälde-Sammlungen, Ausstellung Bayerischer Gemälde des 15. und 16. Jahrhunderts, Munich 1946, p. 4.

301 Will Grohmann, Der blaue Reiter. Gedächtnisausstellung im Haus der Kunst, München, in: Die Neue Zeitung, 7 September 1949.

302 Jella Lepmann, Die Kinderbuchbrücke, op. cit., p. 64. – The exhibition "Books for Young People" was on display in the central section and parts of the west wing from the 3rd to the 31st July. The exhibits formed the basis for the International Youth Library at Kaulbachstrasse 11a formed in 1948. It relocated to Blutenburg Castle near Munich in 1983.

303 Cf. Erste bayerische Exportschau eröffnet, in: Die Neue Zeitung, 27 May 1946.

304 Cf. Erste bayerische Exportschau in München eröffnet, in: Süddeutsche Zeitung, 6 August 1946.

305 Peter A. Ade, Kokoschka und all die anderen, op. cit., p. 35.

306 Chris Dercon / Thomas Weski, foreword to the exhibition, in: Exhibition catalogue Partners, Munich / Cologne 2003, p. 6.

307 Andreas Langenscheidt im Gespräch mit Peter Raue, in: kunst.freunde, edited by the Gesellschaft der Freunde der Stiftung Haus der Kunst München e. V., Munich 2006, p. 51.

308 Exhibition catalogue Entartete Kunst – Bildersturm vor 25 Jahren, Munich 1962, S. VII.

309 Housing the State Gallery of Modern Art in the west wing of Haus der Kunst was considered to be a temporary measure from the very beginning. Since 2002, the collection has been part of the newly constructed Pinakothek der Moderne.

310 Christoph Hackelsberger, Das Steinerne Erbe des Dritten Reiches, in: Süddeutsche Zeitung, 20/21 October 1990.

311 Edith Eiswaldt, Nach dem Verfall der große Knall?, in: Münchner Stadtanzeiger, 25 January 1990.

312 Cf. Das Haus der Kunst bleibt stehen, in: Münchner Merkur, 4 February 1965

313 Rudolf Huber, Haus der Kunst – ein negatives Denkmal, in: Abendzeitung, 13/14 January 1990.

314 Cf. the catalogue to the exhibition Widerstand. Denkbilder für die Zukunft, Ostfildern 1993.

315 Cf. for this, the comments made in the introduction and the details contained in the chronology. In addition: Landbauamt München, Ausarbeitung von Plangutachten zur Gestaltung der freigegebenen Räume zur Verwendung für Tagungen und Veranstaltungen [1959]. Archives of the Bavarian State, MK 51535.

316 Ydessa Hendeles, Partners, in: exhibition catalogue Partners op. cit., p. 18 et seq.

317 His work was on display from March to June 1999 as a temporary installation as part of the "Dream City" group project in which 30 artists participated. "Dream City" was a joint project by Kunstraum München, Museum Villa Stuck and Siemens Kulturprogramm.

[318] Interview with Simone Dattenberger, in: Münchner Merkur, 20 March 1999.

[319] Cf. Sabine Brantl / Ulrich Wilmes, Geschichten im Konflikt: Das Haus der Kunst und der ideologische Gebrauch von Kunst 1937–1955, booklet accompanying the exhibition of the same name, Munich 2012.

[320] Cf. Sabine Brantl: Historisches Archiv Haus der Kunst, in: Der Archivar, Vol. 58 / 2005, Issue 4, p. 280.

Direktor Peter A. Ade (left) with Oskar Kokoschka at Haus der Kunst, 1958

Timeline

1931

Glass Palace at the Old Botanical Gardens burnt to the ground, preliminary project for a new art exhibition building by Prof. Adolf Abel.

1932

Tendering of an architectural competition, first prize to architects Böhm and Feldpausch, Prof. Adolf Abel commissioned for planning

1933

Hitler's "seizure of power". Construction of the "House of German Art" according to plans by Paul Ludwig Troost at a different location in Prinzregentenstrasse, formation of a corporation established under public law named "House of German Art (New Glass Palace)", foundation stone laid on 15 October, Munich given status as "Capital of German Art".

1937

Opening of "House of German Art" on 18 July with the first "Great German Art Exhibition" (held annually until 1944); on 19 July opening of the vilifying show "Degenerate Art" in the neighbouring gallery building at the Hofgarten. The "Great German Art Exhibitions" are considered to be the most important event for the exhibition and sale of works of "German" art and attract several hundred thousand visitors each year.

Exhibition/ Year	**Dates**	**Visitors**
1937	19 Jul 1937 – 31 Oct. 1937	554,759
1938	11 Jul 1938 – 16 Oct. 1938	455,325
1939	17 Jul 1939 – 18 Feb 1940	422,234
1940	27 Jul 1940 – 2 Mar 1941	603,975
1941	27 Jul 1941 – 8 Mar 1942	702,228
1942	4 Jul 1942 – 21 Feb 1943	846,674
1943	26 Jun 1943 – 27 Feb 1944	694,713
1944	26 Jul 1944 – 26 Nov 1944	80,621

there after open on a temporary basis until April 1945

1938

Announcement of a "House of German Architecture" on the occasion of the opening of the second "German Architecture and Handicraft Exhibition" on 10 July.

1945

Orders to hold a further “Great German Art Exhibition” issued by Adolf Hitler on 5 February. US troops enter Munich on 30 April. Requisitioning of the “House of German Art” by the US military government; setting up of an officers mess, Peter A. Ade is appointed trustee.

1946

Renaming of “Haus der Kunst” [House of Art], exhibition “Bavarian Painting in the 15th and 16th Centuries” opened in the west wing with works from the Alte Pinakothek, which had been destroyed; the “Bavarian Export Show” was opened in the east wing.

1948–1982

Peter A. Ade is the director of Haus der Kunst; formation of Ausstellungsleitung München e. V. (renamed “Künstlerverbund im Haus der Kunst München e. V.” in 2014)

1949

Bavarian State Painting Collections are moved to the western section of the building and Ausstellungsleitung e. V. into the eastern section of the building, access through the east wing and west wing, respectively.

1954

Formation of Gesellschaft der Freunde der Ausstellungsleitung Haus der Kunst e. V. (GdF)

1955

Haus der Kunst completely handed back by the military authorities.

1956

Holding of a competition on how to design the rooms being freed up, conversion of the terrace restaurant into exhibition rooms; neutralisation of the “Hall of Honour” (marble pillars painted over, velum installed, walls hung with calico), “P1” studio restaurant moves into the ground flood (later the “P1” disco).

1959

Planting of 16 sycamore trees in front of the southern façade along Prinzregentenstrasse.

1962

The restaurant “Piroschka” moves into the basement (formerly “Bierstüberl”).

1971

Extension of the Altstadtring Nord road link; demolition of the open staircase on Prinzregentenstrasse on account of the road being rerouted, the open staircase is replaced by a central set of steps.

1972

Temporary annexe at the northern end for the exhibition "World Cultures and Modern Art" within the framework of the Olympic Games following a draft by Paolo Nestler.

1980–2000

State Gallery of Modern Art moves into the west wing.

1982–1985

Hermann Kern is director of Ausstellungsleitung e. V.

1985–1990

Magdalena Huber-Ruppel is director of Ausstellungsleitung e. V.

1991 / 1992

Beginning of the renovation work on the eastern section of the building. Formation of Stiftung Haus der Kunst gGmbH on 27 February 1992.

1993–2003

Christoph Vitali is the first director of Stiftung Haus der Kunst.

1994

Reopening of Haus der Kunst on 19 May with the exhibition "Elan Vital or the Eye of Eros".

2001–2007

Establishment of the "Theatre in Haus der Kunst" in the west wing.

2003–2011

Chris Dercon is director of Stiftung Haus der Kunst, Critical Reconstruction.

2005

Opening of the Historical Archive.

since 2011

Okwui Enwezor is director of Stiftung Haus der Kunst.

2013

The internationally renowned architectural office David Chipperfield Architects is awarded the planning contract for the general renovation of Haus der Kunst.

Further reading

Peter A. Ade, Picasso, Kokoschka und all die anderen ... Meine abenteuerlichen Jahre für die Kunst. Nymphenburger Verlag, Munich 2001

"Entartete Kunst". Das Schicksal der Avantgarde im Nazi-Deutschland, ed. Stephanie Barron. Hirmer Verlag, Munich 1992

Haus der Kunst 1937–1997. Ein historische Dokumentation, edited by Sabine Brantl. Haus der Kunst, Munich [1997]

Adolf Hitler, Reden zur Kunst- und Kulturpolitik, ed. Robert Eickmeyer. Revolver Verlag, Frankfurt am Main 2004

Hitlers Künstler. Die Kultur im Dienst des Nationalsozialismus, ed. Hans Sarkowicz. Insel Verlag, Frankfurt am Main / Leipzig 2004

München – "Hauptstadt der Bewegung". Catalogue to the exhibition of the same name held in Munich's museum of city history. Edition Minerva, Munich 2002

Nationalsozialismus und "Entartete Kunst". Die "Kunststadt" München 1937, ed. Peter-Klaus Schuster. Prestel Verlag, Munich 1987

Ort und Erinnerung. Nationalsozialismus in München, ed. Winfried Nerdinger. Verlag Anton Pustet, Salzburg 2006

Paul Ortwin Rave, Kunstdiktatur im Dritten Reich (1949), new ed. Uwe M. Schneede. Argon Verlag, Berlin [1987]

Gavriel D. Rosenfeld, Architektur und Gedächtnis. Dölling und Galitz Verlag, Munich 2004

Eugen Roth, Der Glaspalast in München. Glanz und Ende 1854–1931. Süddeutscher Verlag, Munich 1971

Robert S. Wistrich, Ein Wochenende in München. Kunst, Propaganda und Terror im Dritten Reich. Insel Verlag, Munich 1996

Picture credits

Bayerische Staatsbibliothek, Munich: 30, 32, 35, 38, 53, 54, 78, 79, 83, 85, 101, 114 and cover
Bayerische Staatsgemäldesammlungen, Munich: 121 (photo: Gottfried Schneider)
Bildarchiv Foto Marburg: 20, 22
Haus der Bayerischen Geschichte, Augsburg: 117
Haus der Kunst, Munich: 63 (photo: Wilfried Petzi), 124–125 (VG Bild-Kunst, Bonn), 126 and 128 (photo: Maximilian Geuter)
Historisches Archiv Haus der Kunst, Munich: 47, 50, 52, 98, 115
Künstlerverbund im Haus der Kunst München (formerly Ausstellungsleitung e. V.: 118–119
Münchner Stadtmuseum: 19, 42–43
Privately owned: 152
Stadtarchiv München: 73, 76, 86, 89, 91, 94, 110–111, 113, 120
Zentralinstitut für Kunstgeschichte, Munich/Photothek: 41, 70, 106, 108

All other illustrations from the author's archive.

No. 12 Arcisstraße

The Palais Pringsheim – The Führerbau – The Amerika Haus – The Hochschule für Musik und Theater (University of Music and Performing Arts)

by Alexander Krause

"I would never have believed that I'd ever address another letter to No. 12 Arcisstraße. For some 50 years it was my grandparents' address." Golo Mann writing to the President of the University of Music and Performing Arts Munich, in 1984 Golo Mann's Pringsheim grandparents resided in a neo-renaissance mansion near the Königsplatz, then No. 12 Arcisstraße. The National Socialists saw in the square's classical setting an appropriate stage for their self-promotions and, in 1937, built two Central Party buildings on the corner of Arcis- and Brienner Straße, the southern one for administration and the northern to serve as the "Führerbau" for Hitler and his staff – the present No. 12 Arcisstraße. After 1945, the former Führerbau firstly housed the "Amerika Haus" Cultural Centre and, from 1957, became the main building of the present-day Munich University of Music and Theatre. In this richly illustrated book Alexander Krause researches the varied history of No. 12 Arcisstraße, which not only forms part of Munich's cultural and intellectual history, but also of a sad chapter of world history. edition monacensia publishes works by Munich writers of the 19th and 20th centuries whose literary works are preserved in the Monacensia Literaturarchiv und Bibliothek. Alongside reprints, it also publishes first editions with introductions by specialist editors. This series includes biographies, exhibition catalogues, and books on Munich and Bavaria. Translated by Christina Noel Malcolm.

84 p., Paperback, ISBN: 978-3-86906-048-4

Cosmopolite Meeting Place and Artists' House

The Villa Waldberta: A Mirror oft the 20th Century

by Tobias Mahl

The Villa Waldberta in Feldafing, positioned high over Lake Starnberg in an expansive park, was built as part of the Höhenberg villa colony in 1901/02. From the beginning the grand residence was a place where cosmopolites and artists met, but it also became politically significant: after the Second World War the villa served as quarters for "Displaced Persons" for many years, providing lodgings for those persecuted by the Nazi regime whose repatriation to their native country was untenable. In 1972, during the Olympic Games in Munich, the then Federal Chancellor Willy Brandt stayed in the villa, where he received international politicians like Georges Pompidou and Henry Kissinger. In 1966 the establishment of a private foundation saw the villa pass into the ownership of the City of Munich. In 1982 the City Council decided to open the Villa Waldberta to international scholarship holders, providing them with free accommodation in the villa and allowing them to work creatively.

152 p., Paperback, ISBN: 978-3-86906-123-8